CW01095767

CONTENTS

The QFT SERIES

In the ever-evolving landscape of education, ensuring that every child receives the support they need to thrive is paramount. The concept of Quality First Teaching (QFT) is at the heart of this mission, aiming to provide inclusive and high-quality education for all students. This series of booklets has been meticulously crafted to serve as a comprehensive guide for educators, particularly those working with Special Educational Needs (SEN) students.

Why These Booklets Have Been Written

The primary purpose of these booklets is to empower educators with practical strategies and insights into implementing QFT effectively in their classrooms. Each booklet addresses specific aspects of QFT, providing detailed guidance, real-world examples, and actionable steps to enhance teaching and learning experiences. Inclusion is not merely a policy but a practice that demands dedication, understanding, and continuous improvement. These booklets have been written to:

- Equip educators with the tools and knowledge to support students effectively.

- Foster an inclusive learning environment where every student feels valued and capable.

- Provide practical strategies that can be easily integrated into daily teaching practices.

List of Booklets in the Series

QFT 0 - Adaptive Teaching (publication August 2024)

QFT 1 - Scaffolding (publication August 2024)

QFT 2 - Teacher Talk and Questions (publication August 2024)

QFT 3 - Inclusive Classrooms (publication September 2024)

QFT 4 - Resources (publication October 2024)

QFT 5 - Reasonable Adjustments (publication November 2024)

QFT 6 - Technology (publication December 2024)

QFT 7 - Assessment (publication January 2025)

QFT 8 - Metacognition (publication February 2025)

QFT 9 - TA Support (publication March 2025)

QFT 10 - Instant Intervention (publication April 2025)

QFT 11 - Behaviour, Expectations and Engagement (publication May 2025)

Additional Resources:

- SENDCO Solutions offers engaging in-person or online training and support.

- SENsible SENCO has a video related to the content of this book.

- A printed version of this book is available to purchase from Amazon or the SENsible SENCO website.

- There is a set of Teacher/Trainer cards to support this content. Designed to be used individually in staff briefings or combined to make a longer training session, they provide a teacher cue card and trainer prompt. These are available from the SENsible SENCO website.

This book (QFT 1 – Scaffolding) is supported by book 0 (Adaptive Teaching), Book 2 (Teacher Talk and Questions) and book 9 (TA Support).

INTRODUCTION

UNDERSTANDING QUALITY FIRST TEACHING

Quality First Teaching (QFT) is a robust educational framework designed to ensure that every student benefits from high-quality instruction from the outset. It involves implementing effective teaching strategies that address the varied needs of learners, promoting an inclusive environment where all students have the opportunity to thrive. QFT highlights the significance of differentiated instruction, formative assessment, and cultivating a positive learning atmosphere.

Within the QFT framework, scaffolding plays a critical role. Scaffolding involves providing temporary support to students to help them achieve a higher level of understanding and skill than they would be able to reach independently. This support is gradually removed as students become more proficient, fostering independence and confidence. Scaffolding techniques include breaking tasks into smaller, manageable steps, offering hints and cues, and providing models or examples.

Incorporating scaffolding into QFT ensures that teaching is not only about delivering content but also about supporting students in their learning journey. This approach helps to create a classroom environment where students feel confident, capable, and motivated to learn.

Importance for SEN Students

Certain groups of students, such as those with Special Educational Needs (SEN), English as an Additional Language (EAL), and those from disadvantaged backgrounds (PP), require tailored scaffolding approaches to meet their specific needs. These students often face unique challenges that can hinder their learning if not properly addressed.

- SEN Students: These students may struggle with cognitive processing, attention, and language comprehension. Effective scaffolding for SEN students involves breaking down tasks into smaller steps, using visual aids, and providing consistent feedback and reinforcement. This approach helps SEN students manage their learning more effectively and achieve success in their tasks.

- EAL Students: English language learners may face difficulties with vocabulary, grammar, and cultural nuances. Scaffolding for EAL students includes using visual supports, providing clear and simple instructions, and linking new information to students' existing knowledge. This helps EAL students better understand and engage with the material.

- PP Students (Pupil Premium): Students from disadvantaged backgrounds may lack access to resources and support outside of school. Scaffolding for PP students includes providing additional resources, creating a supportive classroom environment, and offering explicit instructions and practice opportunities. This support helps PP students build confidence and improve their academic outcomes.

Adapting scaffolding techniques to meet the needs of these specific groups ensures that all students can engage with the material and achieve their full potential.

Goals and Objectives

The aim of this booklet is to equip educators with practical strategies and insights for effectively scaffolding student learning in the classroom. By exploring various techniques and approaches, teachers can develop a toolkit that supports Quality First Teaching and meets the diverse needs of their students.

This booklet is designed to be flexible and user-friendly, allowing readers to dip in and out of chapters as needed. Each chapter focuses on a specific aspect of scaffolding, offering detailed explanations, practical examples, and real-world applications. Whether you are looking to refine your scaffolding techniques, better support SEN students, or enhance your overall teaching strategies, this booklet serves as a valuable resource.

Teachers are encouraged to approach the chapters in any order that makes sense for their individual needs and classroom contexts. By integrating the strategies discussed in this booklet, educators can create more inclusive, engaging, and effective learning environments that support the success of all students.

CHAPTER 1: PURPOSES AND BACKGROUND

DEFINITION OF SCAFFOLDING IN EDUCATION

Scaffolding in education refers to a variety of instructional techniques used to move students progressively toward stronger understanding and, ultimately, greater independence in the learning process. The concept, rooted in the work of developmental psychologist Lev Vygotsky, emphasises the importance of providing students with temporary support structures to facilitate learning. These supports are gradually removed as students develop the necessary skills and confidence to perform tasks independently.

> The term "scaffolding" is borrowed from the construction industry, where it denotes a temporary framework that supports workers as they build or repair a structure. Similarly, in education, scaffolding serves as a temporary aid that supports students as they learn new concepts or skills. Once the learner has mastered these, the scaffolding can be dismantled, allowing the student to work independently.

Scaffolding encompasses various strategies, including direct instruction, modelling, questioning, and feedback. For instance, a teacher might initially demonstrate a problem-solving process (modelling), guide students through similar problems (guided practice), and then gradually reduce assistance as students become more proficient (independent practice). Throughout this process, the teacher provides ongoing feedback and adjusts the level of support based on the student's current needs and performance.

One key aspect of effective scaffolding is the teacher's ability to assess the student's Zone of Proximal Development (ZPD). Vygotsky defined the ZPD as the difference between what a learner can do without help and what they can achieve with guidance and encouragement from a skilled partner. By identifying and targeting the ZPD, educators can tailor their scaffolding efforts to provide optimal support, thereby maximising student learning and development.

Effective scaffolding also involves a responsive and flexible approach, where the teacher continuously monitors student progress and adapts their strategies accordingly. This dynamic process ensures that the support provided is neither too challenging nor too simplistic, thereby maintaining the right balance to promote student growth.

Scaffolding is not limited to one-on-one interactions between teacher and student; it can also be implemented in group settings. Collaborative learning, where peers support one another under the guidance of the teacher, is another form of scaffolding. In such environments, students can benefit from the diverse perspectives and skills of their classmates, further enriching their learning experience.

ENHANCING STUDENT ENGAGEMENT AND MOTIVATION

Scaffolding plays a critical role in enhancing student engagement and motivation. When students are provided with the right amount of support and gradually challenged to achieve more, they become more invested in their learning process. This engagement stems from the scaffolded approach's ability to make learning both accessible and stimulating.

One way scaffolding enhances engagement is through the use of incremental challenges that are within the students' Zone of Proximal Development (ZPD). When tasks are too easy, students may become bored and disengaged. Conversely, tasks that are too difficult can lead to frustration and a sense of defeat. Scaffolding helps to find the sweet spot where tasks are challenging enough to be interesting but not so difficult that they become discouraging. By carefully calibrating the difficulty of tasks, educators can maintain a level of challenge that keeps students motivated and eager to learn.

Scaffolding also supports engagement by providing a clear structure and goals. When students understand the steps they need to take to achieve a learning objective, they are more likely to stay focused and persistent. Breaking down complex tasks into manageable parts allows students to experience success at each step, which reinforces their motivation. For example, in a writing assignment, a teacher might first help students brainstorm ideas, then create an outline, write a draft, and finally revise their work. Each stage of the process is scaffolded, making the overall task less daunting and more engaging.

Additionally, scaffolding techniques often incorporate interactive and collaborative activities, which can significantly boost student motivation. Group work, peer tutoring, and cooperative learning tasks allow students to engage with their peers, share ideas, and support each other's learning. This social interaction not only makes learning more enjoyable but also creates a sense of community and belonging, which are key factors in maintaining motivation. For instance, students working together on a science project might feel a collective sense of accomplishment, enhancing their individual and group motivation.

Scaffolding provides timely and constructive feedback, which is essential for maintaining engagement. When students receive immediate feedback, they can quickly identify and correct mistakes, leading to a sense of progress and achievement. This ongoing feedback loop helps students understand that learning is a process and that making mistakes is a natural part of it. Positive reinforcement through feedback encourages students to keep trying and stay engaged with the material.

The role of scaffolding in differentiating instruction also contributes to heightened engagement and motivation. By tailoring support to individual students' needs, teachers can address diverse learning styles and paces. For example, visual learners might benefit from diagrams and charts, while auditory learners might prefer verbal explanations and discussions. By recognising and accommodating these differences, scaffolding ensures that all students remain engaged and motivated.

Scaffolding helps to build students' self-efficacy and confidence. When students successfully complete scaffolded tasks, they gain a sense of competence and belief in their abilities. This self-efficacy is a powerful motivator, driving students to take on new challenges and persist in the face of difficulties. As they experience a series of small successes, their overall confidence in their ability to learn and succeed increases.

SUPPORTING INDEPENDENT LEARNING AND CRITICAL THINKING

Scaffolding is pivotal in fostering independent learning and critical thinking skills. By gradually shifting responsibility from the teacher to the student, scaffolding equips learners with the tools and confidence needed to tackle problems on their own, fostering a sense of autonomy and intellectual curiosity.

One of the primary ways scaffolding supports independent learning is through the gradual release of responsibility model. In this approach, teachers initially provide a high level of support, which is slowly reduced as students gain proficiency. For example, in teaching a complex mathematical concept, a teacher might first demonstrate the procedure, then solve a few problems together with the class, and finally encourage students to solve similar problems independently. This gradual reduction in support helps students build confidence and develop the skills necessary for independent problem-solving.

Scaffolding also encourages the development of critical thinking by promoting active learning. Instead of passively receiving information, students are engaged in activities that require them to apply, analyse, and synthesise knowledge. For instance, during a history lesson, rather than simply presenting facts, a teacher might use scaffolding techniques to guide students in examining primary sources, drawing connections between historical events, and formulating their interpretations. This approach not only deepens understanding but also cultivates critical thinking skills.

Questioning strategies are another effective scaffolding tool that enhances critical thinking. Teachers can use open-ended questions to prompt students to think deeply about the subject matter. For example, in a literature class, instead of asking students to summarise a story, a teacher might ask, "What motivations drive the protagonist's actions, and how do they change throughout the story?" Such questions require students to engage in higher-order thinking, including analysis, evaluation, and synthesis, which are essential components of critical thinking.

Additionally, scaffolding helps students develop metacognitive skills, which are crucial for independent learning. Metacognition involves thinking about one's own thinking processes, and scaffolding can guide students in developing strategies to monitor and regulate their learning. Teachers might model metacognitive strategies, such as self-questioning or summarising information, and then encourage students to use these strategies independently. For example, before beginning a reading assignment, a teacher might model how to set a purpose for reading and ask predictive questions. Gradually, students learn to employ these strategies on their own, enhancing their ability to plan, monitor, and evaluate their learning processes.

The use of graphic organisers is another scaffolding technique that supports both independent learning and critical thinking. Tools like mind maps, Venn diagrams, and flow charts help students organise and visually represent information, making it easier to understand and analyse complex concepts. For instance, in a science class, a teacher might use a flow chart to help students understand the steps of the scientific method. Once students are familiar with the organiser, they can use it independently to plan and conduct their experiments, thus fostering both independence and analytical thinking.

Scaffolding also plays a critical role in developing problem-solving skills, a key aspect of both independent learning and critical thinking. By presenting students with real-world problems and guiding them through the problem-solving process, teachers help students learn how to approach and resolve issues systematically. For example, in a maths class, a teacher might present a complex word problem and guide students through the steps of identifying relevant information, formulating a plan, and executing that plan. Over time, students learn to apply these problem-solving strategies independently.

BRIDGING GAPS IN STUDENT KNOWLEDGE AND SKILLS

Scaffolding is a powerful educational tool for bridging gaps in student knowledge and skills. It provides tailored support that meets students where they are, helping them progress to where they need to be. By addressing individual learning needs and offering incremental assistance, scaffolding ensures that all students can achieve academic success, regardless of their starting point.

One of the primary ways scaffolding helps bridge gaps is through differentiated instruction. Differentiated instruction involves adapting teaching methods and materials to accommodate the diverse learning needs of students. For example, in a mixed-ability classroom, a teacher might provide additional visual aids and hands-on activities for students who struggle with abstract concepts, while offering advanced problem-solving tasks for those who need more challenge. This approach ensures that each student receives the appropriate level of support to progress in their learning. The key here is that the student is still working towards the same learning objective but they are supported to get there.

Scaffolding also involves breaking down complex tasks into smaller, more manageable steps. This chunking technique helps students build their understanding gradually, reducing the cognitive load and making learning more accessible. For instance, when teaching essay writing, a teacher might first focus on helping students develop a strong thesis statement, then guide them in outlining their arguments, and finally support them in writing and revising their drafts. By scaffolding each stage of the writing process, the teacher ensures that students develop the necessary skills incrementally, filling in any gaps in their understanding along the way.

Additionally, scaffolding often includes the use of explicit instruction and modelling. Teachers can demonstrate specific skills or processes, providing clear examples and explanations before students attempt the tasks independently. For example, in a chemistry class, a teacher might first demonstrate how to conduct a titration experiment, explaining each step in detail. Students can then practice the technique with guidance before performing it independently. This method ensures that students have a solid understanding of the necessary procedures and concepts, helping to bridge any gaps in their knowledge.

Another effective scaffolding strategy is the use of formative assessment and feedback. Formative assessments, such as quizzes, class discussions, and practice exercises, allow teachers to identify areas where students may be struggling. Based on this information, teachers can provide targeted feedback and additional support to address specific gaps. For example, if a teacher notices that several students are having difficulty with a particular math concept, they might provide extra practice problems and offer one-on-one assistance to those who need it. This ongoing assessment and feedback loop helps ensure that gaps in knowledge and skills are identified and addressed promptly.

Peer support and collaborative learning are also valuable scaffolding techniques for bridging gaps. Students often learn effectively from their peers, who can offer explanations and perspectives that resonate with them. In a collaborative learning environment, students can work together on tasks, share their knowledge, and support each other's learning. For example, in a language class, students might work in pairs to practice conversational skills, providing feedback and encouragement to each other. This peer interaction not only reinforces learning but also helps fill in gaps by leveraging the strengths of different students.

Technology can also play a significant role in scaffolding learning to bridge gaps. Educational software and online resources can provide personalised learning experiences, adapting to the needs of individual students. For example, adaptive learning platforms can offer practice exercises tailored to each student's skill level, providing additional support where needed and advancing students when they are ready. This personalised approach ensures that gaps in knowledge and skills are addressed efficiently and effectively.

IMPROVING ACADEMIC PERFORMANCE AND CONFIDENCE

Scaffolding is instrumental in improving academic performance and boosting student confidence. By providing structured support that gradually transitions responsibility to the learner, scaffolding ensures that students not only grasp new concepts but also feel confident in applying them independently. This combination of skill acquisition and confidence-building is key to long-term academic success.

One significant way scaffolding improves academic performance is through targeted instruction that meets students at their current level of understanding. By assessing where each student stands, teachers can provide the appropriate level of challenge and support. This personalised approach prevents students from becoming overwhelmed by material that is too difficult or bored by material that is too easy. For example, in a maths class, a teacher might provide extra practice problems with step-by-step guidance for students struggling with algebraic equations, while offering enrichment activities for those who have already mastered the basics. This ensures that all students are continually progressing and improving their performance.

Another aspect of scaffolding that enhances academic performance is the use of clear, step-by-step instructions and models. When teachers demonstrate how to approach a problem or complete a task, they provide a roadmap for students to follow. This clarity helps students understand the process and reduces the cognitive load, making it easier to grasp complex concepts. For instance, in a science class, a teacher might model the process of conducting an experiment, including how to formulate a hypothesis, set up the apparatus, record observations, and analyse results. By seeing the procedure in action, students can better understand each step and replicate the process independently, leading to improved academic outcomes.

Scaffolding also includes providing timely and specific feedback, which is crucial for academic improvement. Feedback helps students understand what they are doing well and where they need to improve. Constructive feedback guides students in making necessary adjustments and encourages them to keep striving for excellence. For example, after a writing assignment, a teacher might provide detailed comments on a student's use of evidence and argumentation, highlighting strengths and suggesting areas for improvement. This feedback helps students refine their skills and perform better in future assignments.

Furthermore, scaffolding fosters a growth mindset, which is essential for academic success and confidence. A growth mindset, the belief that abilities can be developed through dedication and hard work, encourages students to embrace challenges and persevere in the face of setbacks. Scaffolding supports this mindset by showing students that they can improve with effort and guidance. For example, a teacher might celebrate small successes along the way, such as mastering a particular skill or improving a test score, reinforcing the idea that progress is possible. This positive reinforcement builds students' confidence in their abilities and motivates them to continue working hard.

In addition to improving academic performance, scaffolding significantly boosts student confidence. When students receive the support they need to succeed, they develop a sense of competence and self-efficacy. This confidence is crucial for taking on new challenges and persisting in the face of difficulties. For instance, in a language arts class, a teacher might scaffold a reading comprehension activity by first discussing the main ideas and vocabulary, then guiding students through a series of questions about the text, and finally encouraging independent analysis. As students successfully navigate each step, their confidence grows, making them more likely to engage deeply with future reading tasks.

Group work and collaborative learning, often components of scaffolding, also enhance confidence. When students work together, they can share knowledge and support each other, creating a more inclusive and supportive learning environment. For example, in a social studies project, students might work in groups to research different aspects of a historical event, then present their findings to the class. This collaborative approach allows students to learn from each other, build on their strengths, and feel more confident in their contributions.

Finally, scaffolding helps students develop effective study and problem-solving strategies, which are vital for academic success. By modelling and practicing these strategies in a supported environment, students learn how to approach new tasks and challenges independently. For instance, a teacher might scaffold the use of graphic organisers to help students plan an essay or solve a complex problem. As students become proficient in these strategies, they can apply them independently, leading to better academic performance and increased confidence.

FOSTERING A SUPPORTIVE AND INCLUSIVE CLASSROOM ENVIRONMENT

Scaffolding in education is not only a tool for academic achievement but also a means of fostering a supportive and inclusive classroom environment. By providing tailored support and promoting collaboration, scaffolding helps create a learning space where all students feel valued, included, and capable of success. This inclusive atmosphere is essential for student well-being and optimal learning outcomes.

One of the primary ways scaffolding fosters inclusivity is through differentiated instruction. Differentiated instruction involves tailoring teaching methods and materials to meet the diverse needs of students. This approach ensures that all students, regardless of their background, abilities, or learning styles, receive the support they need to succeed. For example, in a classroom with students who have varying levels of English proficiency, a teacher might use visuals, simplified texts, and bilingual resources to help English language learners understand the material. By addressing the unique needs of each student, scaffolding promotes equity and inclusivity in the classroom.

Scaffolding also encourages a collaborative learning environment, which is vital for inclusivity. Collaborative learning activities, such as group projects and peer tutoring, allow students to work together and learn from one another. This cooperation fosters a sense of community and belonging among students. For instance, in a science class, students might work in small groups to conduct experiments, with each member contributing their strengths to the project. This collaboration helps break down social barriers and encourages students to appreciate diverse perspectives and abilities, creating a more inclusive classroom environment.

Another way scaffolding supports inclusivity is by providing a safe space for students to take risks and make mistakes. In a scaffolded learning environment, mistakes are viewed as opportunities for learning rather than failures. Teachers provide constructive feedback and guidance, helping students understand and correct their errors. This approach builds a culture of trust and respect, where students feel comfortable asking questions and seeking help. For example, in a maths class, a teacher might encourage students to explain their problem-solving processes, even if they make mistakes, and then guide them towards the correct solution. This supportive atmosphere helps students develop confidence and resilience, key components of an inclusive classroom.

Scaffolding also plays a crucial role in building positive teacher-student relationships, which are essential for a supportive learning environment. When teachers provide personalised support and show genuine interest in their students' progress, it fosters trust and respect. For instance, a teacher who regularly checks in with students, offers encouragement, and provides tailored feedback demonstrates a commitment to their success. These positive interactions help students feel valued and supported, contributing to a more inclusive and nurturing classroom climate.

In addition, scaffolding can help address and reduce achievement gaps among students. By providing targeted support to those who need it most, scaffolding ensures that all students have the opportunity to succeed. For example, in a reading class, a teacher might use scaffolding techniques such as guided reading sessions and vocabulary previews for students who struggle with literacy. These targeted interventions help close gaps in knowledge and skills, ensuring that every student can achieve their potential.

Furthermore, scaffolding promotes the development of social and emotional skills, which are crucial for an inclusive classroom environment. Activities that require cooperation, communication, and empathy help students build positive relationships with their peers. For example, in a social studies class, students might engage in role-playing activities to understand different historical perspectives, fostering empathy and respect for diverse viewpoints. By developing these social and emotional skills, students are better equipped to contribute to a supportive and inclusive classroom community.

Scaffolding also encourages student agency and voice, which are important for inclusivity. By involving students in the learning process and encouraging them to take ownership of their education, scaffolding empowers them to become active participants in their learning journey. For example, a teacher might use scaffolded questioning techniques to guide students in developing their inquiries and pursuing their interests. This approach not only enhances engagement but also ensures that all students feel heard and valued.

PROMOTING LIFELONG LEARNING SKILLS

Scaffolding in education is essential for promoting lifelong learning skills, equipping students with the ability to continuously acquire, apply, and adapt knowledge throughout their lives. By fostering critical thinking, problem-solving, self-regulation, and a growth mindset, scaffolding prepares students to navigate the complexities of an ever-changing world.

One of the primary ways scaffolding promotes lifelong learning is by encouraging critical thinking. Through scaffolding techniques such as questioning, prompting, and guided discovery, teachers help students develop the ability to analyse information, evaluate evidence, and draw reasoned conclusions. For example, in a history class, a teacher might scaffold a lesson on historical interpretation by asking students to compare different primary sources and discuss the perspectives they represent. This process not only deepens their understanding of historical events but also hones their ability to think critically about various types of information, a skill that is crucial for lifelong learning.

Scaffolding also supports the development of problem-solving skills, which are essential for lifelong learning. By breaking down complex problems into manageable steps and providing appropriate guidance, teachers help students build a systematic approach to problem-solving. For instance, in a maths class, a teacher might scaffold a complex word problem by first helping students identify the relevant information, then guiding them through the steps of setting up and solving the equation. This structured approach helps students develop a problem-solving mindset that they can apply to a wide range of situations beyond the classroom.

Self-regulation is another key lifelong learning skill that scaffolding helps to cultivate. Self-regulation involves the ability to set goals, monitor progress, and adjust strategies as needed. Scaffolding techniques such as goal-setting, self-assessment, and reflective practices help students develop these skills. For example, a teacher might scaffold a writing project by having students set specific writing goals, regularly check their progress against these goals, and reflect on their writing process. This practice helps students learn how to manage their own learning effectively, an essential skill for lifelong learning.

The promotion of a growth mindset is another crucial aspect of scaffolding that supports lifelong learning. A growth mindset, the belief that abilities can be developed through effort and perseverance, encourages students to embrace challenges and view failures as opportunities for growth. Scaffolding supports this mindset by providing the appropriate level of challenge and support, enabling students to experience success and build resilience. For example, a teacher might scaffold a challenging science experiment by providing step-by-step instructions and offering encouragement and feedback throughout the process. As students successfully complete the experiment, they gain confidence in their abilities and are more likely to take on new challenges in the future.

Scaffolding also enhances metacognitive skills, which are critical for lifelong learning. Metacognition involves thinking about one's own thinking processes and strategies. Teachers can scaffold metacognitive skills by modelling and teaching students how to plan, monitor, and evaluate their learning. For example, a teacher might scaffold a reading comprehension activity by demonstrating how to preview a text, set a purpose for reading, and ask questions during reading to monitor understanding. By practicing these strategies with support, students learn how to regulate their own learning, a vital skill for continuous learning throughout life.

Additionally, scaffolding encourages the development of effective communication and collaboration skills. In a scaffolded learning environment, students often work together on tasks, share ideas, and provide feedback to one another. These collaborative experiences help students develop the ability to communicate clearly, listen actively, and work effectively in teams. For example, in a group project on environmental science, students might collaborate to research different aspects of a topic, share their findings, and create a joint presentation. These skills are essential not only for academic success but also for professional and personal growth throughout life.

Furthermore, scaffolding promotes the use of technology and digital literacy, which are increasingly important for lifelong learning. By integrating technology into scaffolded learning activities, teachers help students become proficient in using digital tools and resources. For example, a teacher might scaffold a research project by guiding students in using online databases, evaluating the credibility of sources, and creating digital presentations. These skills are crucial for navigating the digital world and accessing information and opportunities for learning throughout life.

EXAMPLES OF SUCCESSFUL SCAFFOLDING IN VARIOUS EDUCATIONAL SETTINGS

Scaffolding techniques can be successfully applied across a variety of educational settings, from primary schools to universities, and in diverse subjects ranging from literacy to STEM. By tailoring support to meet the needs of different learners and contexts, educators can enhance understanding, foster independence, and improve academic outcomes. Below are some illustrative examples of successful scaffolding in various educational settings.

Primary Education: Literacy Development

In primary schools, scaffolding is often used to develop literacy skills. One effective strategy is the use of guided reading sessions. In these sessions, a teacher works with a small group of students, providing support as they read and discuss a text. The teacher might begin by introducing the book and discussing its themes and vocabulary. During the reading, the teacher offers prompts and questions to help students make predictions, clarify their understanding, and draw inferences. After reading, the teacher leads a discussion to deepen comprehension and connect the text to students ' experiences. Over time, the level of support is reduced as students become more proficient readers, fostering independence and confidence in their reading abilities.

Secondary Education: Mathematics

In secondary education, scaffolding is essential for helping students grasp complex mathematical concepts. For example, when teaching algebra, a teacher might use a step-by-step approach to introduce new topics. Initially, the teacher demonstrates how to solve a particular type of equation, explaining each step and the rationale behind it. Students then practice similar problems with the teacher's guidance, gradually moving towards solving equations independently. Additionally, the teacher might use visual aids such as graphs and manipulatives to reinforce understanding. This method ensures that students build a solid foundation before progressing to more challenging problems, enhancing their confidence and competence in mathematics.

Higher Education: Research Skills

At the university level, scaffolding can be crucial in developing research skills. Professors might scaffold a research project by breaking it down into manageable stages. Initially, they provide a clear framework for the research process, including how to formulate a research question, conduct a literature review, and collect data. Professors might also provide exemplars of high-quality research papers and offer workshops on specific skills such as data analysis and academic writing. Throughout the project, students receive feedback on their progress, helping them refine their research methods and arguments. This structured support helps students develop the skills and confidence needed to undertake independent research.

STEM Education: Science Experiments

In STEM education, scaffolding is often used to guide students through complex scientific experiments. For instance, in a high school biology class, a teacher might scaffold an experiment on photosynthesis. Initially, the teacher explains the scientific principles behind the experiment and demonstrates the procedure. Students then conduct the experiment in small groups, with the teacher providing guidance and feedback at each stage. By gradually reducing support, students learn to design and carry out experiments independently, enhancing their scientific inquiry skills and understanding of the scientific method.

Language Learning: EAL (English as an Additional Language)

Scaffolding is particularly effective in language learning settings, where students are developing proficiency in a new language. For English as an Additional Language (EAL) learners, teachers might use visual aids, gestures, and simplified language to support comprehension. For example, when teaching vocabulary, a teacher might use flashcards with pictures, provide sentence starters, and model correct pronunciation. Group activities such as role-playing and collaborative storytelling also offer opportunities for learners to practice language skills in a supportive environment. As students become more confident, the teacher gradually introduces more complex language structures and lessens the level of support, promoting independence and fluency.

Vocational Education: Skill-Based Learning

In vocational education, scaffolding helps students acquire practical skills essential for their chosen careers. For example, in a culinary arts program, instructors might scaffold the learning process by first demonstrating how to prepare a specific dish. Students then practice the skills under supervision, receiving feedback on techniques and presentation. Over time, students are encouraged to experiment with variations and develop their own recipes, fostering creativity and independence. This hands-on, scaffolded approach ensures that students gain the confidence and competence needed for professional success.

Special Education: Supporting Diverse Learners

In special education, scaffolding is tailored to meet the unique needs of each student. For instance, a teacher working with students with learning disabilities might use multi-sensory instructional methods to enhance understanding. This could involve using tactile materials, visual aids, and auditory cues to teach new concepts. The teacher provides step-by-step instructions and frequent feedback, adjusting the level of support based on the student's progress. By creating a supportive and adaptable learning environment, scaffolding helps diverse learners achieve their full potential.

IMPACT OF SCAFFOLDING ON DIFFERENT LEARNER GROUPS

Scaffolding is a critical educational strategy that benefits diverse learner groups, including students with Special Educational Needs (SEN) and English as an Additional Language (EAL) learners. By providing tailored support and adjusting the level of assistance according to individual needs, scaffolding ensures that all students can access the curriculum and achieve their full potential.

Special Educational Needs (SEN)

Students with SEN often face unique learning challenges that require specialised instructional approaches. Scaffolding provides these students with the structured support necessary to overcome these challenges and succeed academically.

Individualised Support: For students with learning disabilities, scaffolding can involve breaking tasks into smaller, manageable steps and providing clear, concise instructions. For example, a teacher might scaffold a writing assignment by first helping the student brainstorm ideas, then organise those ideas into an outline, and finally write the draft step-by-step. This approach helps students manage the complexity of the task and reduces feelings of overwhelm.

Multi-Sensory Instruction: Scaffolding can incorporate multi-sensory instructional techniques to support students with different learning styles. For instance, a student with dyslexia might benefit from using visual aids, such as graphic organisers, alongside auditory support, like listening to text-to-speech software. These tools help reinforce learning and provide multiple avenues for understanding the material.

Assistive Technology: The use of assistive technology is another form of scaffolding that can significantly benefit SEN students. Tools such as speech-to-text software, interactive learning apps, and adaptive learning platforms provide personalised support that can accommodate various learning needs. For example, a student with attention deficit hyperactivity disorder (ADHD) might use an app that breaks down tasks into timed intervals, helping them stay focused and on track.

English as an Additional Language (EAL)

EAL learners face the dual challenge of acquiring new content knowledge while simultaneously learning a new language. Scaffolding strategies are essential for supporting these students and ensuring they can fully participate in the classroom.

<u>Visual Supports:</u> Visual aids such as pictures, diagrams, and charts are highly effective scaffolding tools for EAL learners. These supports provide context and help students understand new vocabulary and concepts. For example, a science teacher might use labelled diagrams of plant parts to teach botany, making the content more accessible to EAL students.

<u>Language Scaffolding</u>: Teachers can scaffold language development by using sentence frames, word banks, and language models. For instance, during a writing exercise, a teacher might provide sentence starters like "The main idea is..." or "In conclusion...," which help EAL students structure their thoughts and develop their writing skills in English.

<u>Peer Interaction:</u> Collaborative learning activities that pair EAL students with native speakers can provide valuable language practice in a supportive environment. These interactions allow EAL learners to engage in meaningful conversations, practice new vocabulary, and receive immediate feedback. For example, in a history class, students might work in pairs to discuss historical events, with native speakers helping EAL students navigate complex language.

<u>Scaffolded Reading</u>: To support reading comprehension, teachers can use pre-reading activities, such as discussing key vocabulary and themes, and post-reading activities, such as summarising the text and discussing its implications. These strategies help EAL learners build background knowledge and improve their understanding of the text. For example, before reading a novel, a teacher might introduce the main characters and setting, providing EAL students with the context needed to follow the story.

IMPACT ON ACADEMIC ACHIEVEMENT AND CONFIDENCE

Scaffolding not only improves academic performance for SEN and EAL students but also boosts their confidence and engagement. When students receive the support they need to succeed, they are more likely to participate actively in the classroom and take on new challenges.

Enhanced Understanding:

By providing clear, structured support, scaffolding helps students grasp complex concepts and skills. For example, a maths teacher might scaffold a lesson on fractions by using visual aids and hands-on activities to illustrate the concept, ensuring that all students, including those with SEN or EAL, can understand and apply the material.

Increased Independence: As students become more proficient, scaffolding gradually fades, promoting independence. This transition builds students 'confidence in their abilities and encourages them to take ownership of their learning. For instance, an EAL student who initially relied on sentence frames might eventually write essays independently, demonstrating increased confidence and skill.

Positive Learning Environment:

Scaffolding fosters a supportive and inclusive classroom environment, where all students feel valued and capable. This positive atmosphere enhances student motivation and engagement, contributing to better academic outcomes. For example, a classroom that uses peer tutoring as a scaffolding strategy creates a sense of community and mutual support, benefiting all learners.

In conclusion, scaffolding has a profound impact on different learner groups, particularly SEN and EAL students. By providing tailored support, scaffolding helps these students overcome challenges, improve academic performance, and build confidence. Through strategies such as individualised support, multi-sensory instruction, visual aids, language scaffolding, and peer interaction, scaffolding ensures that all students have the opportunity to succeed in an inclusive and supportive learning environment.

ROLE OF SCAFFOLDING IN PERSONALISED LEARNING

Personalised learning tailors education to meet the unique needs, skills, and interests of each student. Scaffolding plays a crucial role in this approach by providing structured support that helps students progress at their own pace and according to their individual learning paths. By leveraging scaffolding techniques, educators can create more effective and engaging personalised learning experiences.

Customised Support

Scaffolding allows educators to provide customised support that addresses each student's specific learning needs. By assessing students 'current levels of understanding and identifying gaps in their knowledge, teachers can tailor their instruction accordingly. For example, in a personalised learning environment, a teacher might use diagnostic assessments to determine a student's strengths and weaknesses in reading comprehension. Based on the results, the teacher can then provide targeted scaffolding, such as reading materials at the appropriate level, vocabulary support, and guided reading sessions, to help the student improve.

Adaptive Learning Technologies

Technology plays a significant role in personalised learning, and scaffolding can be integrated into adaptive learning platforms. These platforms use algorithms to adjust the difficulty and type of content based on the student's performance. For instance, a maths learning app might offer more challenging problems as a student demonstrates proficiency, while providing additional hints and simpler problems when the student struggles. This real-time adjustment ensures that each student receives the appropriate level of challenge and support, facilitating personalised learning pathways.

Self-Paced Learning

Scaffolding supports self-paced learning, a key component of personalised learning. Students can progress through the curriculum at their own speed, with scaffolding providing the necessary guidance to ensure they master each concept before moving on. For example, in a blended learning environment, students might use online modules to learn new content. Teachers can scaffold this process by providing checklists, progress trackers, and periodic assessments to help students stay on track and identify areas where they need additional support. This approach allows students to take ownership of their learning and move forward when they are ready.

Differentiated Instruction

Differentiated instruction is a core principle of personalised learning, and scaffolding is essential in implementing it effectively. Teachers can use scaffolding to differentiate their instruction based on students 'learning styles, interests, and abilities. For instance, in a project-based learning scenario, a teacher might scaffold the process by providing different levels of support for different students. Visual learners might receive graphic organisers and diagrams, while kinaesthetic learners might engage in hands-on activities. By differentiating instruction through scaffolding, teachers can ensure that all students are engaged and able to succeed in their personalised learning journeys.

Promoting Student Autonomy

Scaffolding helps develop the skills and confidence students need to become autonomous learners, a primary goal of personalised learning. By gradually reducing support as students become more proficient, scaffolding encourages independent problem-solving and critical thinking. For example, in a science class, a teacher might initially guide students through the steps of the scientific method with detailed instructions and examples. As students become more familiar with the process, the teacher gradually reduces the level of guidance, encouraging students to design and conduct their experiments independently. This progression fosters autonomy and prepares students for lifelong learning.

Enhancing Engagement and Motivation

Personalised learning aims to increase student engagement and motivation by aligning education with students 'interests and goals. Scaffolding supports this by making learning more accessible and manageable. When students receive the right amount of support, they are more likely to experience success and stay motivated. For instance, in a personalised writing program, a teacher might scaffold the process by helping students select topics that interest them, providing graphic organisers for planning, and offering feedback on drafts. This personalised support makes the writing process more engaging and rewarding for students, enhancing their motivation to learn.

Real-World Application and Skill Development

Scaffolding in personalised learning often involves connecting classroom learning to real-world contexts and applications. This approach helps students see the relevance of their education and develop practical skills. For example, in a personalised learning environment focused on career readiness, a teacher might scaffold a project where students explore different professions. The teacher could provide initial support by helping students research career options, arrange job shadowing experiences, and develop resumes. As students gain experience and confidence, the scaffolding is gradually removed, allowing them to take more responsibility for their learning and career planning.

Continuous Feedback and Reflection

Scaffolding incorporates continuous feedback and reflection, which are essential for personalised learning. By providing ongoing feedback, teachers help students understand their progress, identify areas for improvement, and adjust their learning strategies. For instance, in a personalised maths program, a teacher might use formative assessments to monitor student progress and provide feedback on specific skills. Students can then reflect on their performance, set goals, and make necessary adjustments. This iterative process of feedback and reflection helps students take control of their learning and fosters continuous improvement.

Collaborative Learning Opportunities

While personalised learning often focuses on individual progress, scaffolding can also facilitate collaborative learning opportunities. By working together on scaffolded tasks, students can share their knowledge, support each other, and develop important social skills. For example, in a personalised history project, students might work in small groups to research and present on different historical events. The teacher can scaffold this collaboration by providing guidelines, roles, and checkpoints to ensure effective teamwork. This approach combines the benefits of personalised learning with the advantages of collaborative learning, enhancing both individual and group outcomes.

Supporting Diverse Learners

Scaffolding is particularly effective in supporting diverse learners within a personalised learning framework. Whether students have special educational needs, are English language learners, or come from different cultural backgrounds, scaffolding can provide the customised support they need to succeed. For example, a personalised learning program for EAL students might include scaffolded language support, such as vocabulary previews, language models, and interactive activities. This targeted support helps EAL students access the curriculum and develop their language skills, ensuring that personalised learning is inclusive and equitable.

History and theoretical backgrounds

ORIGIN OF SCAFFOLDING CONCEPT: JEROME BRUNER AND LEV VYGOTSKY

The concept of scaffolding in education has its roots in the pioneering work of Lev Vygotsky and Jerome Bruner, both of whom significantly advanced our understanding of how learners acquire new skills and knowledge through guided support.

Lev Vygotsky

Lev Vygotsky, a Soviet psychologist, focused on the social aspects of learning and the importance of interactions between learners and more knowledgeable others. Central to Vygotsky's theory is the concept of the Zone of Proximal Development (ZPD), which he defined as the difference between what a learner can do independently and what they can achieve with guidance and support from a skilled partner (Vygotsky, 1978). Vygotsky believed that learning occurred most effectively within this zone, as the support provided by the more knowledgeable other enables the learner to perform tasks they would not be able to complete alone.

Jerome Bruner

Jerome Bruner, an American psychologist, expanded on Vygotsky's ideas and was instrumental in popularising the concept of scaffolding in the context of education. Bruner's work in the 1960s and 1970s emphasised the importance of structure in learning and the role of teachers in guiding and supporting students' learning processes. He introduced the term "scaffolding" to describe the temporary support structures that teachers provide to help students achieve higher levels of understanding and skill (Bruner, 1976). These supports are gradually removed as students become more competent, allowing them to perform tasks independently.

Bruner's approach to scaffolding was closely tied to his theories on discovery learning, which advocate for a learning environment where students are encouraged to explore, experiment, and discover new concepts with the teacher's guidance. He argued that this method helps students develop critical thinking skills and a deeper understanding of the material. According to Bruner, effective scaffolding involves not only providing support but also engaging students in the learning process and encouraging active participation (Bruner, 1961).

Integration of Vygotsky and Bruner's Ideas

The integration of Vygotsky and Bruner's ideas forms the basis of the modern understanding of scaffolding in education. While Vygotsky provided the theoretical framework with his ZPD concept, Bruner offered practical insights into how scaffolding could be implemented in educational settings. Together, their work highlights the importance of social interaction, guidance, and the gradual transfer of responsibility from teacher to student.

In practice, scaffolding involves various techniques such as modelling, questioning, providing feedback, and breaking down tasks into smaller, manageable steps. These techniques are designed to support students as they work within their ZPD, gradually building their competence and confidence until they can perform tasks independently.

VYGOTSKY'S ZONE OF PROXIMAL DEVELOPMENT (ZPD)

Lev Vygotsky's concept of the Zone of Proximal Development (ZPD) is a cornerstone of his socio-cultural theory of learning and development. The ZPD is defined as the gap between what a learner can accomplish independently and what they can achieve with the guidance and support of a more knowledgeable other, such as a teacher, peer, or parent (Vygotsky, 1978).

Theoretical Foundations of ZPD

Vygotsky's ZPD is rooted in the idea that social interaction plays a fundamental role in cognitive development. Unlike Piaget, who emphasised stages of individual development, Vygotsky argued that learning is inherently a social process, mediated by language and interaction with others. He posited that children internalise the knowledge and skills demonstrated by others through these interactions, which then become part of their cognitive framework.

The ZPD represents a dynamic and fluid range of abilities, not fixed stages of development. It acknowledges that learning is most effective when it occurs just beyond the learner's current level of competence, where they can be challenged yet still successful with appropriate support. This concept has profound implications for educational practice, suggesting that teaching should be tailored to the learner's current developmental level while also pushing them toward higher levels of understanding.

APPLICATION OF ZPD IN EDUCATION

The practical application of the ZPD in education involves identifying the learner's current abilities and providing appropriate scaffolding to support their progress. Scaffolding refers to the temporary support structures that enable learners to perform tasks they cannot yet complete independently. These supports are gradually removed as the learner gains competence, promoting independence and self-efficacy (Wood, Bruner, & Ross, 1976).

For instance, in a classroom setting, a teacher might use a variety of scaffolding techniques such as:

1. Modelling: Demonstrating a task or skill, which the student then attempts to replicate.

2. Prompting and Cueing: Providing hints or questions that guide the learner toward the solution.

3. Think-Alouds: Verbalising thought processes while performing a task to model cognitive strategies.

4. Feedback: Offering constructive feedback to help learners correct errors and refine their understanding.

By using these strategies, teachers can help students navigate their ZPD, gradually increasing the complexity of tasks as students develop their skills and knowledge.

Implications for Differentiated Instruction

Vygotsky's ZPD also underscores the importance of differentiated instruction, where teaching methods and materials are adapted to meet the diverse needs of learners. Recognising that each student has a unique ZPD, educators can tailor their scaffolding strategies to provide the right level of challenge and support for each individual. This approach ensures that all students are engaged and making progress, regardless of their starting point.

For example, in a reading lesson, a teacher might use different texts and scaffolding techniques based on students' reading levels. Beginners might work with simpler texts and receive more direct support, such as pre-teaching vocabulary and frequent comprehension checks, while more advanced readers might tackle complex texts with minimal support, focusing on higher-order skills like analysis and interpretation.

ZPD and Collaborative Learning

Vygotsky also highlighted the role of collaborative learning in the ZPD. He believed that learners benefit from working with peers, as this interaction can provide opportunities for mutual scaffolding. In collaborative settings, students can share knowledge, ask questions, and offer explanations, helping each other move through their respective ZPDs.

For instance, in a group project, students with different strengths and knowledge levels can collaborate to complete a task. More knowledgeable students can support their peers, while all group members contribute to the collective learning process. This peer interaction not only enhances understanding but also builds communication and teamwork skills.

KEY THEORIES INFLUENCING SCAFFOLDING: CONSTRUCTIVISM, SOCIAL CONSTRUCTIVISM

The educational concept of scaffolding is deeply rooted in the theoretical frameworks of Constructivism and Social Constructivism. These theories provide the philosophical and psychological underpinnings for understanding how scaffolding facilitates learning by supporting the learner's construction of knowledge through guided interactions.

Constructivism

Constructivism, primarily associated with Jean Piaget, posits that learners construct their own understanding and knowledge of the world through experiences and reflecting on those experiences. According to Piaget, learning is an active process where students build new knowledge upon the foundation of their previous knowledge (Piaget, 1952).

Piaget's stages of cognitive development outline how children move through different stages of understanding as they grow. Constructivist teaching strategies, therefore, emphasise the importance of providing experiences that are appropriate to the learner's current stage of cognitive development. In this context, scaffolding can be seen as a way to provide the necessary support to help learners move from one stage to the next. By breaking down complex tasks into manageable parts and providing guidance and support, teachers help students build on their existing knowledge and reach higher levels of understanding.

For example, in a constructivist classroom, a teacher might introduce a new concept in mathematics by first connecting it to concepts the students are already familiar with. The teacher then guides the students through a series of increasingly challenging problems, providing hints and feedback as needed, until the students can solve the problems independently. This scaffolding process helps students construct a deeper understanding of the new concept based on their existing knowledge.

Social Constructivism

Social Constructivism, advanced by Lev Vygotsky, expands on the ideas of Constructivism by emphasising the critical role of social interaction and cultural context in the construction of knowledge. Vygotsky argued that cognitive development is largely a socially mediated process, where learning occurs through interactions with others who are more knowledgeable (Vygotsky, 1978).

Central to Social Constructivism is the concept of the Zone of Proximal Development (ZPD), which Vygotsky defined as the difference between what a learner can do independently and what they can achieve with guidance and support from a more knowledgeable other. Scaffolding is a direct application of this theory, as it involves providing the support needed to help learners accomplish tasks within their ZPD.

In practice, social constructivist approaches to scaffolding involve collaborative learning activities, peer tutoring, and guided instruction. For instance, in a language arts class, students might work in pairs or small groups to discuss a text. The teacher facilitates the discussion by posing open-ended questions and encouraging students to think critically about the text. More knowledgeable peers can support those who are struggling, providing explanations and insights that help them understand the material. Over time, as students gain confidence and understanding, the teacher gradually reduces the level of support, encouraging students to take on more responsibility for their learning.

Integration of Theories in Scaffolding

The integration of Constructivist and Social Constructivist theories in scaffolding highlights the importance of both individual cognitive processes and social interactions in learning. Effective scaffolding requires understanding the learner's current knowledge and developmental stage (Constructivism) and providing appropriate social support and guidance to extend that knowledge (Social Constructivism).

For example, a science teacher might use constructivist principles to design a lab activity that builds on students' prior knowledge of chemical reactions. The teacher then uses social constructivist strategies to facilitate group work, where students collaborate to design and conduct experiments. Throughout the process, the teacher provides scaffolding by modeling scientific inquiry, asking probing questions, and offering feedback. This combined approach helps students construct new knowledge through active engagement and social interaction.

THE ROLE OF THE TEACHER AS A FACILITATOR

In the context of scaffolding, the teacher's role transitions from a traditional instructor to a facilitator of learning. This shift is essential for effectively supporting student-centred learning environments where students are actively engaged in constructing their knowledge with the teacher's guidance.

Guiding the Learning Process

As facilitators, teachers guide the learning process rather than simply delivering information. This involves diagnosing the learner's current level of understanding, identifying gaps, and providing appropriate scaffolding to bridge those gaps. The teacher assesses students' prior knowledge and skills to tailor instruction that challenges them within their Zone of Proximal Development (ZPD) (Vygotsky, 1978).

For example, in a mathematics class, a teacher might begin by assessing students' understanding of fundamental algebraic concepts. Based on this assessment, the teacher can then design activities that provide just enough support to help students grasp more complex algebraic operations. This might involve working through problems step-by-step, using visual aids, or providing concrete examples that make abstract concepts more accessible.

Providing Scaffolding

Providing scaffolding involves a variety of strategies that support students as they develop new skills and understandings. Effective scaffolding techniques include:

1. Modelling: Demonstrating a task or process so that students can observe the steps involved and understand the thought process behind it. For instance, a teacher might model how to approach a complex text by thinking aloud while reading, highlighting how to infer meaning from context clues and questioning the text.

2. Questioning: Asking strategic questions that prompt students to think critically and reflect on their learning. Open-ended questions encourage deeper thinking and exploration of the subject matter. For example, in a history lesson, a teacher

might ask, "What might have motivated this historical figure to take these actions?"

3. Providing Feedback: Offering timely and specific feedback that helps students understand their errors and how to improve. Feedback should be constructive and aimed at guiding students toward self-correction and deeper understanding. For instance, in a writing assignment, a teacher might highlight areas where the argument is strong and suggest ways to improve weaker sections.

4. Using Visual Aids and Tools: Incorporating visual aids, such as charts, diagrams, and graphic organisers, to help students visualise relationships and concepts. In a science class, a teacher might use a flowchart to explain the steps of the scientific method, helping students understand the sequence and purpose of each step.

Encouraging Independence

A key aspect of the facilitator role is gradually transferring responsibility to the learner. As students become more proficient, the teacher reduces the level of support, encouraging students to take more control over their learning. This process, known as "fading," helps students develop confidence and autonomy.

For example, in a project-based learning environment, a teacher might initially provide detailed instructions and close supervision. As students gain experience and skills, the teacher steps back, allowing students to plan and execute their projects more independently. This not only builds students 'problem-solving and critical thinking skills but also fosters a sense of ownership and motivation.

Creating a Collaborative Learning Environment

Facilitators also create and maintain a collaborative learning environment where students feel comfortable sharing ideas and working together. This involves fostering a classroom culture of respect, openness, and mutual support. Teachers encourage peer interactions and group work, where students can learn from one another and support each other's learning.

For instance, in a language arts class, a teacher might organise literature circles where small groups of students read and discuss a novel together. The teacher facilitates the discussions by providing guiding questions and ensuring that all students participate, but the focus is on student-led dialogue and exploration of the text.

Adapting to Individual Needs

Effective facilitators are responsive to the diverse needs of their students. They adapt their scaffolding techniques based on individual learning styles, preferences, and progress. This involves being flexible and attentive, ready to adjust the level and type of support as needed.

For example, in a mixed-ability classroom, a teacher might use differentiated instruction strategies to provide varying levels of scaffolding. Advanced students might be given more challenging tasks with less direct support, while struggling students receive additional guidance and resources. This ensures that all students are appropriately challenged and supported in their learning journey.

In summary, the role of the teacher as a facilitator in the context of scaffolding is multifaceted, involving guiding the learning process, providing targeted support, encouraging independence, fostering collaboration, and adapting to individual needs. By adopting this approach, teachers can create dynamic and supportive learning environments that empower students to reach their full potential.

EVOLUTION OF SCAFFOLDING PRACTICES OVER TIME

The concept and practice of scaffolding in education have evolved significantly since their inception, reflecting changes in educational theories, technological advancements, and an increased understanding of student learning processes. This evolution underscores the dynamic nature of teaching methodologies and their adaptation to meet diverse learner needs.

Early Foundations

The early foundations of scaffolding were laid by Lev Vygotsky in the early 20th century, with his introduction of the Zone of Proximal Development (ZPD) (Vygotsky, 1978). Vygotsky's ideas emphasised the importance of social interaction and guidance in learning. Jerome Bruner further expanded these concepts in the 1960s and 1970s, coining the term "scaffolding" to describe the temporary supports provided by teachers to help students achieve higher levels of understanding (Bruner, 1976).

During this period, scaffolding was primarily conceptualised within the context of direct teacher-student interactions. Teachers would model tasks, provide hints and cues, and gradually withdraw support as students became more competent. This approach was revolutionary at the time, shifting the focus from rote memorisation to a more interactive and student-centred learning process.

Development in Pedagogical Approaches

In the latter part of the 20th century, educational research and pedagogical approaches began to incorporate more structured and diverse scaffolding techniques. This period saw the integration of various instructional strategies, such as differentiated instruction and formative assessment, which complemented the scaffolding framework.

For example, in the 1980s and 1990s, educators began to emphasise the importance of formative assessments—ongoing evaluations of student understanding that inform instructional adjustments. Formative assessments allowed teachers to provide more targeted and effective scaffolding by identifying specific areas where students needed support (Black & Wiliam, 1998).

Additionally, the concept of "gradual release of responsibility" became a central theme in scaffolding practices. This approach involves a systematic shift from teacher-led instruction to student independence, encapsulated in the "I do, we do, you do" model. This method ensures that students gradually take on more responsibility for their learning, with the teacher providing decreasing levels of support as competence increases (Pearson & Gallagher, 1983).

Technological Advancements

The advent of digital technology in the late 20th and early 21st centuries brought significant changes to scaffolding practices. Technology has provided new tools and platforms for delivering and enhancing scaffolding in educational settings. Online learning environments, interactive software, and digital resources have expanded the ways in which scaffolding can be implemented.

For instance, adaptive learning technologies use algorithms to tailor educational content to individual student needs in real-time. These platforms adjust the difficulty of tasks based on student performance, providing personalised scaffolding that can help students stay within their ZPD. Examples include educational software like Khan Academy and intelligent tutoring systems that offer hints and feedback based on student responses (Kulik & Fletcher, 2016).

Furthermore, technology has facilitated collaborative learning environments through online discussion forums, virtual classrooms, and social media platforms. These tools enable peer scaffolding, where students support each other's learning through interaction and collaboration, often with teacher facilitation (Means et al., 2010).

Contemporary Practices

In contemporary educational settings, scaffolding practices continue to evolve, integrating insights from cognitive science, educational psychology, and technology. Current trends emphasise the importance of metacognitive strategies, where students are taught to think about their thinking processes and become more self-regulated learners.

Modern scaffolding practices also focus on creating more inclusive learning environments that address the needs of diverse student populations, including those with special educational needs (SEN) and English as an Additional Language (EAL) learners. Teachers use a variety of scaffolding techniques, such as visual aids, differentiated tasks, and cooperative learning, to ensure that all students have access to the support they need (Gibbons, 2015).

In addition, there is a growing emphasis on culturally responsive scaffolding, which takes into account students' cultural backgrounds and experiences in the learning process. This approach recognises the importance of culturally relevant teaching materials and methods that resonate with students' lived experiences, thereby enhancing engagement and learning outcomes (Gay, 2018).

Future Directions

Looking ahead, the evolution of scaffolding practices is likely to continue as educational research and technology advance. Emerging fields such as artificial intelligence and data analytics hold promise for developing even more sophisticated and personalised scaffolding tools. These technologies could provide real-time insights into student learning patterns and offer targeted interventions that are precisely tailored to individual needs.

Moreover, as the understanding of how students learn continues to deepen, educators will be better equipped to design and implement scaffolding strategies that are both effective and equitable. This ongoing evolution underscores the dynamic nature of education and the continuous quest to support all learners in achieving their full potential.

INTEGRATION OF SCAFFOLDING IN CONTEMPORARY EDUCATIONAL THEORIES

Scaffolding is deeply embedded in contemporary educational theories, reflecting its importance in effective teaching and learning. These theories, which include Constructivism, Social Constructivism, and Connectivism, emphasise the role of scaffolding in facilitating student learning through guided support, collaboration, and the use of technology.

Constructivism

Constructivist theory, influenced by Jean Piaget, posits that learners construct knowledge through their experiences and interactions with the world. In this framework, scaffolding is seen as essential for helping learners build upon their existing knowledge and understanding. Teachers act as facilitators, providing the necessary support to help students navigate new concepts and ideas (Piaget, 1952).

In practice, constructivist approaches to scaffolding involve creating learning experiences that are student-centred and inquiry-based. For example, a science teacher might design a series of hands-on experiments that build on students' prior knowledge of scientific principles. The teacher provides initial guidance and support, gradually reducing assistance as students develop a deeper understanding and ability to conduct experiments independently.

Social Constructivism

Social Constructivism, advanced by Lev Vygotsky, emphasises the importance of social interactions and cultural context in the learning process. Scaffolding, in this context, involves collaborative learning and guided support from teachers and peers. The Zone of Proximal Development (ZPD) is central to Social Constructivism, highlighting the range within which learning occurs most effectively with the right level of support (Vygotsky, 1978).

Scaffolding in social constructivist classrooms often includes group work, peer tutoring, and cooperative learning activities. For instance, in a literature class, students might work in small groups to analyse a complex text. The teacher facilitates discussions and provides prompts to guide analysis, allowing more knowledgeable peers to support those who are less confident. Over time, the teacher gradually reduces support, encouraging students to take more responsibility for their learning.

Connectivism

Connectivism, a relatively new educational theory developed by George Siemens and Stephen Downes, focuses on the role of technology and networks in learning. It posits that learning occurs across a network of connections, both digital and social, and that the ability to navigate these networks is crucial for acquiring knowledge (Siemens, 2005).

In a connectivist framework, scaffolding involves using technology to provide personalised and adaptive support. Educational technologies, such as learning management systems (LMS), online forums, and digital collaboration tools, facilitate scaffolding by offering resources, feedback, and opportunities for interaction. For example, an online course might use adaptive learning software that adjusts the level of difficulty based on student performance, providing hints and resources when needed.

Integration in Curriculum Design

Contemporary curriculum design increasingly incorporates scaffolding as a foundational element. Educators design curricula that include structured support mechanisms to help students progress from basic to advanced levels of understanding. This approach ensures that all students, regardless of their starting point, receive the support they need to succeed.

For example, in a mathematics curriculum, lessons might be sequenced to gradually increase in complexity. Each lesson builds on the previous one, with scaffolded activities that help students master foundational skills before moving on to more challenging concepts. Teachers use formative assessments to gauge student understanding and adjust scaffolding as needed to support individual learning trajectories.

Professional Development and Teacher Training

The integration of scaffolding in contemporary educational theories also extends to teacher professional development and training programs. Educators are trained to use scaffolding techniques effectively, learning how to provide appropriate support, diagnose student needs, and gradually transfer responsibility to learners.

Professional development programs often include workshops, peer observations, and reflective practice sessions where teachers can develop and refine their scaffolding skills. For instance, teachers might participate in collaborative planning sessions where they design scaffolded lesson plans, share strategies, and receive feedback from colleagues.

Scaffolding and Inclusive Education

Inclusive education aims to provide equitable learning opportunities for all students, including those with diverse learning needs. Scaffolding is a critical strategy in inclusive education, as it allows teachers to differentiate instruction and provide tailored support to students with varying abilities.

In an inclusive classroom, scaffolding might involve using visual aids, differentiated tasks, and assistive technologies to support students with disabilities. For example, a teacher might use graphic organisers and step-by-step instructions to help a student with a learning disability understand a complex concept. This approach ensures that all students have access to the curriculum and can achieve their full potential.

Global Perspectives on Scaffolding

Scaffolding practices vary across different educational systems and cultural contexts, but the underlying principles remain consistent. Educators worldwide recognise the value of scaffolding in promoting student learning and engagement. In some countries, scaffolding is integrated into national curriculum frameworks, while in others, it is emphasised through teacher training and professional development programs.

For example, in Finland, a country renowned for its high-performing education system, scaffolding is an integral part of the teaching and learning process. Finnish educators use a variety of scaffolding techniques to support student learning, including personalised instruction, formative assessment, and collaborative learning activities (Sahlberg, 2011).

INFLUENTIAL STUDIES AND RESEARCH ON SCAFFOLDING

Scaffolding has been a focal point in educational research, with numerous studies examining its effectiveness and applications in diverse learning contexts. This body of research provides a robust evidence base that supports the integration of scaffolding in teaching practices. Below are some of the most influential studies and research findings on scaffolding.

Wood, Bruner, and Ross (1976)

One of the seminal studies on scaffolding was conducted by David Wood, Jerome Bruner, and Gail Ross in 1976. Their research introduced the concept of scaffolding and described its essential features. They highlighted six key functions of scaffolding: recruiting the learner's interest, reducing the degrees of freedom in the task, maintaining goal orientation, highlighting critical features, controlling frustration, and demonstrating idealised versions of the task (Wood, Bruner & Ross, 1976). This study laid the groundwork for understanding how scaffolding can support learning processes and has been widely cited in subsequent research.

Collins, Brown, and Newman (1989)

In their influential work on cognitive apprenticeship, Collins, Brown, and Newman (1989) explored how scaffolding can be used to teach complex cognitive skills. They emphasised the importance of making thinking visible through modelling, coaching, and scaffolding. Their research demonstrated that scaffolding helps learners develop problem-solving skills and cognitive strategies that are essential for mastering complex tasks. This work expanded the application of scaffolding beyond basic skill acquisition to higher-order cognitive processes.

Palincsar and Brown (1984)

Ann Brown and Annemarie Palincsar's study on Reciprocal Teaching (1984) is another cornerstone in scaffolding research. They developed a teaching method where students and teachers take turns leading discussions about text, using four key strategies: summarising, questioning, clarifying, and predicting. Their research showed that this scaffolded approach significantly improved students 'reading comprehension and metacognitive skills (Palincsar & Brown, 1984). The success of Reciprocal Teaching provided strong evidence for the effectiveness of scaffolding in promoting deeper understanding and active learning.

Rosenshine and Meister (1992)

Rosenshine and Meister (1992) conducted a meta-analysis of studies on scaffolding techniques, particularly focusing on the use of scaffolding in teaching reading comprehension strategies. Their analysis found that scaffolded instruction, such as providing prompts, cues, and feedback, was highly effective in helping students develop comprehension skills. They concluded that scaffolding is a critical component of effective reading instruction, helping students navigate and make sense of complex texts.

Van de Pol, Volman, and Beishuizen (2010)

In a comprehensive review of the scaffolding literature, Van de Pol, Volman, and Beishuizen (2010) synthesised findings from numerous studies to identify key characteristics of effective scaffolding. They highlighted the importance of contingency, fading, and transfer of responsibility in scaffolding. Their review reinforced the idea that scaffolding should be responsive to the learner's needs and should gradually transfer control from the teacher to the student. This review provided a detailed framework for implementing scaffolding in various educational contexts (Van de Pol, Volman & Beishuizen, 2010).

Hammond and Gibbons (2005)

Jennifer Hammond and Pauline Gibbons (2005) explored the use of scaffolding in language learning, particularly for English as an Additional Language (EAL) students. They identified specific scaffolding strategies that support language development, such as using visual aids, modelling language structures, and providing sentence starters.

Their research demonstrated that scaffolding is crucial for helping EAL students access the curriculum and develop proficiency in the target language. This work has had significant implications for teaching practices in linguistically diverse classrooms.

Hattie (2009)

John Hattie's meta-analysis in *Visible Learning* (2009) synthesised over 800 meta-analyses relating to achievement. Hattie identified scaffolding as one of the most effective teaching strategies, with a high impact on student learning. He emphasised that effective scaffolding involves clear instruction, timely feedback, and opportunities for students to practice new skills in a supportive environment. Hattie's work underscored the importance of scaffolding in promoting student achievement across different subjects and educational levels.

Sawyer (2006)

Keith Sawyer's research on the creative learning environments highlighted the role of scaffolding in fostering creativity and problem-solving. Sawyer argued that scaffolding is essential for guiding students through the creative process, helping them generate ideas, explore possibilities, and refine their solutions. His work demonstrated that scaffolding can be used not only for traditional academic subjects but also for promoting innovation and creativity in various domains (Sawyer, 2006).

Saye and Brush (2002)

John Saye and Thomas Brush (2002) investigated the use of scaffolding in inquiry-based learning environments. They developed a model of "soft" and "hard" scaffolds to support students in complex inquiry tasks. "Soft" scaffolds are dynamic and responsive, provided by teachers during the learning process, while "hard" scaffolds are static supports, such as guides and tools, designed into the learning environment. Their research showed that a combination of both types of scaffolding effectively supports students 'inquiry skills and knowledge construction.

Belland, Kim, and Hannafin (2013)

Brian Belland, ChanMin Kim, and Michael Hannafin (2013) conducted a meta-analysis on the effects of computer-based scaffolding in STEM education. Their findings indicated that digital scaffolding tools, such as simulations, interactive software, and online tutorials, significantly enhance students' problem-solving abilities and conceptual understanding in STEM subjects. This research highlighted the potential of technology to provide scalable and personalised scaffolding in modern classrooms.

COMPARATIVE ANALYSIS OF SCAFFOLDING ACROSS DIFFERENT EDUCATIONAL SYSTEMS

Scaffolding as an educational strategy has been implemented and adapted across various educational systems worldwide, reflecting diverse cultural, pedagogical, and policy contexts. This comparative analysis examines how scaffolding is applied in different countries, highlighting similarities, differences, and the impact on student learning.

Finland: Individualised Support and Student-Centred Learning

Finland is renowned for its high-performing education system, which emphasises student-centred learning and individualised support. Finnish educators integrate scaffolding into their teaching practices by providing tailored support to meet the diverse needs of students. This approach involves formative assessments, personalised feedback, and differentiated instruction.

Finnish teachers are well-trained in recognising each student's Zone of Proximal Development (ZPD) and designing scaffolded activities that promote gradual skill acquisition. Collaborative learning is also a key component, with students working in small groups to support each other's learning. This method fosters a supportive classroom environment where students are encouraged to take ownership of their learning (Sahlberg, 2011).

Japan: Lesson Study and Collaborative Planning

In Japan, scaffolding is often integrated into the teaching practice through the concept of "Lesson Study," a collaborative professional development approach where teachers jointly plan, observe, and analyse learning and teaching in 'research lessons.' This practice allows teachers to develop and refine scaffolded instruction techniques collectively.

Japanese educators emphasise the gradual release of responsibility, where students move from guided practice to independent work. Teachers use scaffolding techniques such as questioning, prompting, and modelling to support student learning. Additionally, the cultural emphasis on effort and perseverance aligns well with the scaffolding approach, encouraging students to persist through challenges with appropriate support (Takahashi & Yoshida, 2004).

Singapore: Mastery Learning and Systematic Scaffolding

Singapore's education system is known for its structured and systematic approach to teaching and learning, particularly in STEM subjects. Scaffolding in Singaporean schools often involves "mastery learning," where students must achieve a high level of understanding before moving on to more complex topics.

Teachers in Singapore provide scaffolding through clear, step-by-step instructions, regular feedback, and targeted interventions for students who struggle. This approach ensures that all students have a solid foundation before progressing, reducing knowledge gaps and promoting a deep understanding of the material. Technology is also widely used to provide personalised scaffolding, such as through adaptive learning platforms and interactive digital resources (Ng, 2008).

United States: Differentiated Instruction and Inclusive Practices

In the United States, scaffolding is an integral part of differentiated instruction and inclusive education practices. Teachers use a variety of scaffolding strategies to accommodate the diverse needs of students, including those with special educational needs (SEN) and English as an Additional Language (EAL) learners.

American educators often employ scaffolding techniques such as visual aids, graphic organisers, and collaborative learning activities. The use of technology, such as educational software and online resources, provides additional support and personalisation. The emphasis on formative assessment and data-driven instruction helps teachers identify students' needs and adjust scaffolding accordingly (Tomlinson, 2001).

China: Teacher-Centred Scaffolding with High Expectations

In China, education is characterised by a strong emphasis on teacher-directed instruction and high academic expectations. Scaffolding in Chinese classrooms often involves explicit teaching and systematic practice, with teachers providing detailed explanations and demonstrations.

Chinese educators use scaffolding techniques such as repetition, guided practice, and continuous assessment to ensure students master foundational skills. The cultural value placed on education and respect for teachers supports this structured approach, fostering an environment where students are motivated to excel with the guidance of their teachers (Wang & Peverly, 1986).

Comparative Insights and Implications

While scaffolding practices vary across different educational systems, several common themes emerge:

1. Adaptation to Cultural Contexts: Scaffolding techniques are adapted to fit the cultural and pedagogical contexts of each country. For example, the collaborative and reflective nature of Lesson Study in Japan aligns with the cultural emphasis on collective effort and improvement.

2. Emphasis on Individualised Support: Regardless of the system, effective scaffolding involves recognising individual student needs and providing tailored support. This approach is evident in Finland's personalised learning strategies, Singapore's mastery learning model, and the differentiated instruction practices in the United States.

3. Integration of Technology: Many educational systems leverage technology to enhance scaffolding. Adaptive learning platforms, digital resources, and online collaboration tools provide scalable and personalised support for students.

4. Professional Development: Continuous professional development is crucial for effective scaffolding. Practices like Japan's Lesson Study and the professional learning communities in the United States help teachers refine their scaffolding techniques and share best practices.

5. Focus on Formative Assessment: Formative assessment is a key component of scaffolding, allowing teachers to monitor student progress and adjust support as needed. This practice is widely used across different systems to ensure that scaffolding is responsive and effective.

Scaffolding is a versatile and effective instructional strategy that has been adapted to various educational systems worldwide. By tailoring support to meet the diverse needs of students, scaffolding promotes deeper understanding, skill acquisition, and academic success. The comparative analysis of scaffolding practices across different countries highlights the importance of cultural context, individualised support, technology integration, professional development, and formative assessment in implementing effective scaffolding strategies.

CRITICISMS AND LIMITATIONS OF SCAFFOLDING

While scaffolding is widely regarded as an effective educational strategy, it is not without its criticisms and limitations. These challenges highlight the complexity of implementing scaffolding effectively and underscore the need for careful consideration and adaptation in educational contexts.

Dependency on the Teacher

One significant criticism of scaffolding is that it can foster dependency on the teacher if not implemented correctly. Students who become accustomed to constant guidance and support may struggle to transition to independent learning. This issue arises when scaffolding is not gradually withdrawn as students gain competence, leading to a situation where learners rely excessively on the teacher for assistance.

To mitigate this, educators must carefully balance support and independence, ensuring that scaffolding is gradually reduced to promote self-reliance. Effective scaffolding involves a planned approach to fading support, allowing students to develop confidence and skills necessary for independent problem-solving and learning.

Time-Consuming Nature

Scaffolding can be time-consuming for both teachers and students. Providing individualised support, continuous feedback, and adjusting instructional strategies require significant time and effort. In classrooms with large student-to-teacher ratios, it can be challenging for educators to provide adequate scaffolding for all students.

This limitation suggests the need for efficient planning and use of resources. Teachers can employ peer scaffolding, where more knowledgeable students support their peers, and use technology to provide additional resources and feedback. These strategies can help distribute the scaffolding workload and ensure that all students receive the support they need.

Difficulty in Implementation

Implementing scaffolding effectively requires a high level of skill and understanding from educators. Teachers must be adept at diagnosing students 'current levels of understanding, providing appropriate support, and adjusting scaffolding as students progress. This complexity can make scaffolding challenging to implement, particularly for less experienced teachers.

Professional development and ongoing training are crucial to address this issue. Educators need opportunities to learn about scaffolding techniques, practice them in their classrooms, and receive feedback on their implementation. Collaborative professional learning communities can also provide support and share best practices.

Potential for Misalignment with Curriculum Standards

Another criticism is that scaffolding may sometimes conflict with standardised curriculum and assessment requirements. In educational systems that emphasise high-stakes testing and rigid curricula, there may be limited flexibility to provide the individualised support that scaffolding requires. This misalignment can hinder the effective implementation of scaffolding.

To address this, educational policymakers and curriculum developers need to recognise the value of scaffolding and create frameworks that allow for flexible, student-centred teaching practices. Integrating scaffolding into curriculum standards can help ensure that it is seen as a fundamental part of the teaching and learning process, rather than an add-on.

Challenges in Measuring Effectiveness

Measuring the effectiveness of scaffolding can be challenging due to its dynamic and individualised nature. Traditional assessment methods may not capture the incremental progress that students make with scaffolding. Additionally, the impact of scaffolding may vary widely depending on the context and implementation.

To overcome this, educators and researchers need to develop assessment tools that can accurately measure the outcomes of scaffolded instruction. Formative assessments, portfolios, and performance-based assessments can provide a more comprehensive picture of student progress and the effectiveness of scaffolding.

Risk of Over-Scaffolding

Over-scaffolding occurs when teachers provide too much support, preventing students from engaging in productive struggle and developing critical thinking skills. This can limit students' opportunities to learn from mistakes and discover solutions independently.

Educators must find a balance between providing necessary support and encouraging independent thinking. This involves recognising when to step back and allow students to take risks, make errors, and learn from the process. Encouraging a growth mindset and resilience in students can help them navigate challenges with confidence.

Cultural and Contextual Considerations

Scaffolding strategies may not always transfer seamlessly across different cultural and educational contexts. What works in one setting might not be effective in another due to varying cultural norms, educational practices, and student expectations. For example, a highly structured scaffolding approach may not align well with educational systems that prioritise student autonomy and inquiry-based learning.

Educators need to adapt scaffolding techniques to fit the cultural and contextual needs of their students. This involves being culturally responsive, understanding the backgrounds and experiences of learners, and modifying scaffolding strategies to ensure they are relevant and effective.

Despite its limitations, scaffolding remains a powerful instructional strategy that can significantly enhance student learning when implemented effectively. Addressing the criticisms and challenges of scaffolding requires careful planning, professional development, and a flexible approach that considers the unique needs of students and educational contexts. By doing so, educators can harness the full potential of scaffolding to support student growth and achievement.

CHAPTER 2: TYPES AND PRINCIPLES OF SCAFFOLDING

Scaffolding in education is a pivotal concept that plays a crucial role in supporting student learning and development. This chapter delves into the various types of scaffolding and the guiding principles that underpin their effective implementation. Scaffolding refers to the temporary support provided to students to help them achieve a higher level of understanding and skill than they would be able to reach independently. As students become more proficient, this support is gradually removed, fostering autonomy and self-reliance.

The types of scaffolding explored in this chapter include soft scaffolding, such as hints and prompts, and hard scaffolding, including templates and checklists. Additionally, the chapter examines peer scaffolding, where collaborative learning enhances understanding, and technological scaffolding, which leverages digital tools to enrich the educational experience. Content-specific scaffolding and dynamic, adaptive methods that adjust to student progress are also discussed, highlighting the diverse approaches educators can employ to meet varied learning needs.

Principles of effective scaffolding are essential to guide its application in educational settings. Understanding student needs and prior knowledge forms the foundation of tailored support. Setting clear and achievable learning goals provides direction, while the gradual release of responsibility—moving from instructor-led to student-led activities—encourages independence. Providing timely and constructive feedback, fostering metacognition, and creating a supportive learning environment are critical to maintaining engagement and promoting self-regulation. Balancing challenge with support ensures that students remain motivated, while continuous assessment allows for the adjustment of strategies to suit evolving learner requirements. Integrating scaffolding with other instructional approaches, such as Universal Design for Learning (UDL) and differentiated instruction, further enhances its effectiveness.

SOFT VS. HARD SCAFFOLDING

Definitions and Distinctions

Scaffolding in education is an instructional strategy that involves providing temporary support to students to facilitate their learning. This support is gradually removed as students become more competent, enabling them to achieve independence in their learning process. Scaffolding can be broadly categorised into two types: soft scaffolding and hard scaffolding.

Soft scaffolding refers to the more flexible, adaptive, and often spontaneous forms of support provided during the learning process. It includes techniques such as hints, prompts, and encouragement that help guide students' thinking and problem-solving efforts. Soft scaffolding is typically verbal and can be adjusted in real-time based on the student's immediate needs.

Hard scaffolding, on the other hand, involves more structured and pre-planned supports. These are often tangible resources or tools such as templates, checklists, and models. Hard scaffolding is designed to provide a clear framework or pathway for students to follow, offering concrete examples or steps that can guide their learning process.

Examples of Soft Scaffolding

1. Hints: Providing subtle clues that nudge students toward discovering the solution to a problem on their own. For example, in a maths class, a teacher might hint at the next step in solving an equation without giving away the answer.

2. Prompts: Asking guiding questions that encourage students to think critically and reflect on their understanding. For instance, a teacher might ask, "What do you think will happen if we change this variable?" to stimulate analytical thinking.

3. Encouragement: Offering positive reinforcement and motivational support to build students' confidence and perseverance. This might involve praising effort, highlighting progress, or reassuring students that making mistakes is a natural part of learning.

Examples of Hard Scaffolding

1. Templates: Providing students with pre-designed formats or outlines that they can use to organise their work. For example, an essay template that includes sections for introduction, body paragraphs, and conclusion helps students structure their writing.

2. Checklists: Offering a list of criteria or steps that students can follow to ensure they complete a task correctly. In a science project, a checklist might include items such as "formulate a hypothesis," "conduct the experiment," and "record results."

3. Models: Demonstrating a process or providing an example of a finished product that students can emulate. A teacher might show a model of a completed maths problem or a well-structured piece of writing to illustrate what is expected.

When to Use Soft vs. Hard Scaffolding

The choice between soft and hard scaffolding depends on various factors, including the learning objectives, the complexity of the task, and the individual needs of the students.

Soft scaffolding is particularly useful in situations where:

-   The learning task requires higher-order thinking skills and creativity.

-   Students need to develop problem-solving strategies and critical thinking.

-   The teacher wants to foster independence and self-regulation in students.

For example, during a group discussion on a complex topic, a teacher might use soft scaffolding to prompt students to share their ideas and build on each other's thoughts, encouraging deeper engagement and collaborative learning.

Hard scaffolding is more appropriate when:

-   The task is complex and students need a clear, structured pathway to follow.

-   Students are learning new content or skills that require a foundational understanding.

-   The teacher aims to ensure that all students meet specific criteria or standards.

For instance, in a writing assignment, providing a template can help students organise their thoughts and ensure they include all necessary components, thereby reducing cognitive load and allowing them to focus on the content of their writing.

Ultimately, effective scaffolding often involves a combination of both soft and hard approaches. Teachers need to assess the needs of their students and the demands of the task to provide the most appropriate type of support. As students gain proficiency, the scaffolding can be gradually withdrawn, empowering them to become more autonomous and confident learners.

PEER SCAFFOLDING

Definition and Significance

Peer scaffolding involves students supporting each other's learning through collaborative interactions. In this approach, peers provide assistance, guidance, and encouragement, often taking on roles traditionally held by teachers. This method capitalises on the social and cognitive benefits of peer interactions, allowing students to work together to understand concepts, solve problems, and complete tasks. The significance of peer scaffolding lies in its ability to foster a dynamic and interactive learning environment, promoting a sense of community and shared responsibility for learning.

Vygotsky's concept of the "more knowledgeable other" (MKO) is foundational to understanding peer scaffolding. According to Vygotsky, learning occurs within the Zone of Proximal Development (ZPD), where students can perform a task under adult guidance or with peer collaboration that they could not achieve alone. The MKO is any individual who possesses a higher level of knowledge or skill than the learner, and in peer scaffolding, students often alternate being the MKO. This dynamic allows students to benefit from each other's strengths, making the learning process more reciprocal and inclusive. Peer work leverages the MKO concept by encouraging students to teach and learn from each other, thereby deepening their understanding and fostering mutual growth.

Benefits of Peer Interactions and Collaborative Learning

Peer scaffolding offers numerous benefits that enhance both academic and social outcomes for students. Firstly, it promotes enhanced understanding. When students explain concepts to their peers, they reinforce their own understanding and identify any gaps in their knowledge. This process of teaching others requires clarity of thought and often leads to a deeper comprehension of the subject matter.

Secondly, peer interactions increase engagement. Collaborative activities are generally more stimulating and enjoyable, which boosts students' motivation and interest in the subject. This increased engagement can lead to higher levels of participation and effort in learning activities.

Thirdly, peer scaffolding helps develop essential social skills. Students learn to communicate effectively, listen actively, and negotiate different viewpoints. These skills are crucial for their overall development and future interactions in various contexts.

Peer scaffolding also encourages critical thinking. Exposure to diverse perspectives and problem-solving approaches stimulates students' analytical abilities. They must evaluate different ideas, integrate new information, and develop well-rounded solutions to problems.

Additionally, peer interactions build confidence. Successfully helping peers can boost students' self-efficacy and confidence in their abilities. This supportive environment encourages risk-taking and resilience, as students feel more comfortable making mistakes and learning from them.

Lastly, peer scaffolding fosters a collaborative culture within the classroom. This culture of mutual support and cooperation can lead to sustained academic and social benefits, creating a positive and inclusive learning environment.

Strategies for Implementing Peer Scaffolding Effectively

To implement peer scaffolding effectively, educators can employ several strategies. One key approach is to structure group work carefully. Organising students into small groups with clear roles and responsibilities ensures that each member contributes to the group's success. Regularly rotating these roles can give all students opportunities to lead and support, enhancing their collaborative skills.

Peer tutoring is another effective strategy. Pairing students of different ability levels allows more knowledgeable students to assist those who need extra help. This can be done informally during class activities or through structured programmes where students meet regularly to review material.

Collaborative projects also facilitate peer scaffolding. Designing projects that require students to work together towards a common goal ensures that they rely on each other's strengths and knowledge. Clear guidelines on task division and integration of contributions are essential for the success of such projects.

The think-pair-share technique is a simple yet powerful method to promote peer learning. This involves asking students to think about a question individually, then discussing it with a partner, and finally sharing their ideas with the larger group. This method encourages active participation and helps students refine their thoughts through peer interaction.

Incorporating peer review and feedback sessions can also enhance peer scaffolding. Teaching students how to give and receive constructive feedback based on specific criteria promotes critical thinking and self-assessment skills. This process helps improve the quality of students' work and their ability to critique constructively.

Cooperative learning activities, such as the jigsaw method, are particularly effective. In this approach, students are divided into groups where each member is responsible for learning and teaching a different section of the material. This ensures that all students contribute and learn from each other, promoting a comprehensive understanding of the topic.

Leveraging technology can further facilitate peer scaffolding. Online discussion forums, collaborative documents, and educational platforms enable students to interact and support each other beyond the classroom. These tools can make peer scaffolding more accessible and flexible, accommodating different learning styles and schedules.

TECHNOLOGICAL SCAFFOLDING

Role of Digital Tools and Resources

Digital tools and resources have revolutionised modern education by offering scalable and adaptable scaffolding to support diverse learning needs. Technological scaffolding involves the use of educational software, online platforms, and interactive simulations to enrich the learning experience. These tools can personalise learning paths, provide immediate feedback, and grant access to a vast array of resources, thereby supporting students in ways that traditional methods may not. The integration of technology in education aligns with Vygotsky's theory of the Zone of Proximal Development (ZPD), where digital tools can function as the "more knowledgeable other," offering tailored support to each learner.

Educational Software, Online Platforms, Interactive Simulations

Educational software such as Khan Academy and Duolingo offers structured learning experiences that adapt to the user's pace and level of understanding. These platforms include interactive exercises, quizzes, and progress tracking, helping students master specific skills at their own speed. Online platforms like Moodle, Canvas, and Google Classroom facilitate the organisation and delivery of educational content, enabling teachers to assign tasks, share resources, and communicate with students in a cohesive learning environment. Interactive simulations, such as those provided by PhET Interactive Simulations and Labster, allow students to engage with complex scientific concepts through virtual experiments. These simulations enable hands-on learning experiences that are often difficult to replicate in traditional classroom settings, enhancing both engagement and comprehension.

Benefits and Challenges of Technological Scaffolding

The benefits of technological scaffolding are multifaceted. One significant advantage is personalisation and adaptivity. Digital tools can tailor learning experiences to individual students 'needs, providing customised feedback and support, which aligns with Vygotsky's ZPD. Immediate feedback is another key benefit, as many educational technologies offer real-time responses, helping students correct mistakes and understand concepts instantly. Cognitive science research underscores the importance of timely feedback in reinforcing learning and aiding memory retention.

Accessibility and inclusivity are further benefits, with technological tools making learning more accessible to students with diverse needs, including those with disabilities. Features such as text-to-speech, subtitles, and adjustable text sizes support Universal Design for Learning (UDL) principles, ensuring all students can engage with the material. Additionally, the interactive and multimedia-rich content of digital tools can enhance student engagement and motivation. Gamification elements, like badges and leaderboards, make learning more enjoyable and incentivise progress.

However, technological scaffolding also presents challenges. The digital divide remains a significant issue, as not all students have equal access to technology and the internet, potentially exacerbating existing educational inequalities. Furthermore, technology can sometimes lead to distractions, with students veering off-task, and there is a risk of overreliance on digital aids, which may impede the development of independent learning skills. Quality and effectiveness vary widely among educational software and resources, necessitating critical evaluation by educators to ensure they are pedagogically sound. Technical issues, such as software glitches or connectivity problems, can disrupt the learning process and cause frustration.

Best Practices for Integrating Technology in Scaffolding

To effectively integrate technology in educational scaffolding, it is essential to align digital tools with learning goals. Technology should enhance, rather than replace, traditional instructional methods, supporting specific educational objectives. Providing adequate training and support for both teachers and students is crucial for effective use. Ongoing professional development and technical support can help educators seamlessly incorporate technology into their teaching practices.

Monitoring and evaluating the effectiveness of digital tools is necessary to ensure they positively impact student learning outcomes. Data and feedback should inform decisions about which tools to continue using and which to modify or replace. Fostering digital literacy among students is also important, teaching them to use technology responsibly and effectively, including aspects of digital citizenship, online safety, and critical evaluation of digital content.

Balancing technology with traditional methods can help mitigate the challenges associated with overreliance on digital tools. A blended approach that combines both can provide a more comprehensive educational experience.

CONTENT-SPECIFIC SCAFFOLDING

Tailoring Scaffolding Techniques to Different Subjects

Content-specific scaffolding involves tailoring instructional support to the unique demands and characteristics of different subject areas. This approach recognises that various disciplines require different types of thinking, skills, and knowledge, and therefore, the scaffolding strategies must be adapted accordingly. Effective content-specific scaffolding helps students engage more deeply with the material, promotes better understanding, and enhances overall learning outcomes.

Subject-Specific Examples and Strategies

> STEM (Science, Technology, Engineering, Mathematics)

In STEM subjects, scaffolding often focuses on developing problem-solving skills, analytical thinking, and the application of theoretical concepts to practical scenarios.

1. Science: In a biology class, scaffolding might include the use of graphic organisers to help students map out complex processes such as photosynthesis. Teachers can provide step-by-step guides for conducting experiments, along with pre-lab questions to prepare students for hands-on activities. Additionally, virtual labs and simulations can be used to visualise processes that are difficult to observe directly.

2. Mathematics: For mathematics, scaffolding could involve breaking down complex problems into smaller, more manageable steps. Teachers might use visual aids like number lines, graphs, and manipulatives to illustrate abstract concepts. Providing worked examples followed by guided practice helps students gradually take on more challenging problems independently.

3. Engineering: In engineering courses, project-based learning can be scaffolded through design templates, checklists for project phases, and peer review sessions to critique and improve designs. Simulations and modelling software can provide practical insights and allow students to experiment with different engineering solutions in a controlled environment.

4. Technology: For technology subjects, scaffolding might include tutorials and interactive modules that guide students through coding exercises or software

usage. Providing sample codes, troubleshooting tips, and collaborative projects can help students build technical skills incrementally.

Humanities

In the humanities, scaffolding focuses on developing critical thinking, interpretation, and communication skills.

1. **Literature:** In literature classes, scaffolding could involve using reading guides that help students identify themes, character development, and literary devices. Teachers might use discussion prompts and Socratic questioning to encourage deeper analysis and interpretation of texts. Graphic organisers can also help students structure their essays and arguments effectively.

2. **History:** For history, timelines, and concept maps can be used to scaffold the understanding of historical events and their relationships. Primary source analysis guides can help students critically evaluate historical documents. Teachers might provide structured essay outlines to assist students in organising their research and arguments coherently.

3. **Languages:** In language learning, scaffolding could include vocabulary lists, sentence starters, and conversation scripts to support speaking and writing exercises. Interactive language apps and games can reinforce grammar and vocabulary skills in an engaging way. Role-playing and dialogue practice can also be scaffolded through guided scenarios and feedback sessions.

4. **Philosophy:** In philosophy courses, scaffolding might involve providing frameworks for logical argumentation and ethical analysis. Teachers can use case studies and thought experiments to prompt critical thinking and discussion. Structured debates and reflective journals can help students articulate and refine their philosophical positions.

Impact on Student Outcomes in Various Disciplines

Content-specific scaffolding has a profound impact on student outcomes across different disciplines. In STEM fields, tailored scaffolding enhances students' ability to solve complex problems, apply theoretical knowledge to real-world situations, and develop critical thinking skills. Research indicates that students who receive structured

73

support in STEM subjects show improved performance, greater retention of material, and increased interest in pursuing STEM careers.

In the humanities, effective scaffolding fosters deeper comprehension, critical analysis, and effective communication. Students develop the ability to interpret texts, construct coherent arguments, and engage in thoughtful discussions. This leads to improved writing skills, better performance on assessments, and a greater appreciation for the subject matter.

DYNAMIC AND ADAPTIVE SCAFFOLDING

Definition and Characteristics

Dynamic and adaptive scaffolding refers to a flexible and responsive approach to instructional support that evolves based on students' progress and changing needs. Unlike static scaffolding, which is predetermined and fixed, dynamic scaffolding adjusts in real-time, responding to the learner's current performance, understanding, and engagement levels. This approach is characterised by its fluidity, continuous assessment, and customisation, ensuring that each student receives the appropriate level of support at the right time. The core attributes of dynamic scaffolding include responsiveness to learners, personalisation of support, ongoing assessment, and the use of timely feedback loops to guide learning.

It is similar to hard and soft scaffolding but is approached more dynamically.

Methods for Adjusting Scaffolding Based on Student Progress

To effectively implement dynamic and adaptive scaffolding, educators can employ several key methods. Formative assessment is central to this process, as it involves regularly using tools like quizzes, exit tickets, and observational checklists to gauge students' understanding and skills. These assessments provide valuable data that can inform necessary adjustments to scaffolding strategies. Differentiated instruction is another essential method, involving the adaptation of instruction to meet the diverse needs of students by offering varying levels of support, different tasks, and alternative resources. This ensures that all students can access the curriculum at their level of readiness.

Real-time feedback is crucial for dynamic scaffolding, providing immediate responses during learning activities. For example, during a writing exercise, a teacher might circulate the classroom to offer on-the-spot suggestions and corrections based on students' current work. Interactive technology also plays a significant role, with adaptive learning technologies like DreamBox and Smart Sparrow automatically adjusting task difficulty based on student performance. These tools personalise learning experiences by continuously analysing student responses and adapting accordingly.

Scaffold fading is a method where support is gradually reduced as students become more competent. Initially, substantial support is provided, which is then slowly removed as the learner gains confidence and proficiency, encouraging independent problem-solving and self-regulation. Peer-assisted learning further facilitates dynamic scaffolding by leveraging the assistance of more knowledgeable students, who can provide adaptive support to their peers based on ongoing needs.

Benefits of Dynamic Scaffolding for Diverse Learners

Dynamic and adaptive scaffolding offers significant benefits, particularly for diverse learners with varying backgrounds, abilities, and learning styles. This approach enhances engagement by providing tailored support that matches students' immediate needs, keeping tasks at an optimal level of difficulty. By continuously adjusting support based on real-time data, dynamic scaffolding helps address learning gaps promptly, leading to better understanding and retention of material, and ultimately improving learning outcomes.

For diverse learners, including those with special educational needs, English language learners, and gifted students, personalised scaffolding caters to individual learning preferences and paces, ensuring that all students can succeed. This tailored approach fosters the development of self-regulation skills as scaffold fading encourages students to take ownership of their learning and become independent learners. As students build confidence and resilience, they are better prepared for future academic challenges.

CHAPTER 3: INTRODUCTION TO MODELLING:

Modelling is a pivotal instructional strategy in education, serving as a cornerstone of effective teaching and learning. It involves the teacher demonstrating a task or process to the students, providing a clear and concrete example of what is expected. This method allows students to observe and understand the steps involved in completing a task, thus making abstract concepts more accessible and comprehensible. By observing the teacher's actions and thought processes, students can learn not only the 'what' but also the 'how' and 'why' behind various tasks and concepts.

The effectiveness of modelling lies in its ability to make invisible cognitive processes visible. It offers students a window into the expert thinking and strategies used by their teacher, which they can then emulate and internalise. This approach is beneficial across all educational levels and subjects, from primary school to higher education, and from literacy to mathematics, science, and the arts.

In this chapter, we will explore several key aspects of modelling as a scaffolding strategy. We will begin by examining how demonstrating tasks and processes can provide students with clear, step-by-step guidance. Next, we will delve into think-aloud strategies, which involve the teacher verbalising their thought processes to illustrate cognitive strategies and problem-solving approaches. We will then discuss the benefits of modelling for student understanding, highlighting how this technique can enhance comprehension, reduce anxiety, and foster independent learning. Finally, we will provide examples of effective modelling across different subjects, showcasing its versatility and applicability in various educational contexts.

DEMONSTRATING TASKS AND PROCESSES

Demonstrating tasks and processes is a fundamental component of modelling, a critical scaffolding strategy in education. This approach involves the teacher performing a task in front of the students, providing a live, step-by-step example of how to achieve a specific outcome. Through demonstration, students can see exactly what is expected of them and understand the nuances of completing a task. This chapter delves into the importance, methods, and benefits of demonstrating tasks and processes, with examples across various subjects.

The Importance of Demonstration

Demonstration plays a crucial role in bridging the gap between abstract concepts and practical application. It allows students to observe the detailed process involved in completing a task, which is especially beneficial for complex or unfamiliar activities. By watching a teacher model a task, students can visualise the steps, understand the sequence of actions, and see the application of theoretical knowledge in a real-world context. This method of instruction aligns with the principles of social learning theory, which emphasises the importance of observing and imitating the behaviours of others (Bandura, 1977).

Methods of Effective Demonstration

To maximise the effectiveness of demonstrations, teachers should consider several key strategies:

1. Clear and Structured Steps: Break down the task into manageable steps and present them in a logical sequence. Each step should be clearly explained and visibly demonstrated. For instance, when teaching how to solve a quadratic equation, a teacher might start by identifying the standard form of the equation, then move on to factoring, applying the quadratic formula, and finally solving for the variable.

2. Verbal Explanations: Accompany each action with a verbal explanation to reinforce understanding. Explain the purpose of each step, the reasoning behind

it, and any common pitfalls to avoid. For example, in a cooking class, a teacher might explain why it is essential to preheat the oven before baking.

3. Visual Aids: Use visual aids such as diagrams, charts, and handouts to complement the demonstration. These aids can help visual learners grasp the information more effectively. In a biology class, a teacher might use a diagram of the human body while demonstrating a dissection.

4. Interactive Elements: Encourage student interaction during the demonstration. Ask questions, invite predictions, and allow students to participate in certain steps. This engagement can enhance understanding and retention. For instance, in a chemistry lesson, a teacher might ask students to predict the outcome of a chemical reaction before demonstrating it.

5. Reflective Pause: Periodically pause during the demonstration to check for understanding and address any questions. This ensures that students are following along and provides an opportunity to clarify any confusion.

Benefits of Demonstrating Tasks and Processes

The benefits of demonstrating tasks and processes are manifold:

1. Enhanced Comprehension: Demonstration provides a concrete example that students can follow, making it easier to understand complex or abstract concepts. By seeing each step in action, students can better grasp the procedures and underlying principles involved.

2. Increased Engagement: Watching a live demonstration can be more engaging than passive forms of instruction, such as lectures or reading assignments. It captures students' attention and maintains their interest, particularly when the demonstration involves hands-on or interactive elements.

3. Skill Acquisition: Demonstration is particularly effective for teaching practical skills that require precise techniques, such as laboratory procedures, artistic methods, or athletic movements. By observing the teacher's actions, students can learn the correct techniques and avoid developing bad habits.

4. Confidence Building: Seeing a task successfully completed by the teacher can boost students' confidence in their ability to perform the task themselves. This

confidence can reduce anxiety and increase their willingness to attempt challenging activities.

5. Differentiated Instruction: Demonstrations can be adapted to meet the needs of diverse learners. Visual learners benefit from seeing the process, auditory learners from hearing the explanations, and kinesthetic learners from participating in the demonstration.

Examples of Demonstration Across Subjects

- Mathematics: In a mathematics class, a teacher might demonstrate how to solve a complex equation on the board. They could start by outlining the equation, then methodically solve it step-by-step, explaining each action. This could involve simplifying expressions, combining like terms, and isolating the variable. By seeing the entire process, students can understand the logical progression and the rationale behind each step.

- Literacy: In a literacy lesson, a teacher could model the process of writing an essay. They might begin by brainstorming ideas, then create an outline, write a thesis statement, and draft the introduction. Each part of the essay-writing process would be demonstrated, with explanations of why each step is important and how it contributes to the overall structure of the essay.

- Science: In a science class, a teacher might demonstrate an experiment, such as a chemical reaction. They would explain the hypothesis, outline the materials needed, and then perform the experiment while discussing each step. This might include measuring chemicals, mixing solutions, and observing the results. The teacher could also demonstrate how to record observations and analyse the data.

- History: In a history lesson, a teacher might demonstrate how to analyse a primary source document. They could start by providing context about the document, then read it aloud while highlighting significant passages. The teacher might model how to ask critical questions about the source, such as the author's perspective, the historical context, and the intended audience.

- Art: In an art class, a teacher might demonstrate a particular painting technique. They could start by preparing the materials, then show how to mix colours, apply brush strokes, and create different textures. The teacher would explain the techniques and principles behind each action, allowing students to understand and replicate the process.

Demonstrating tasks and processes is a powerful scaffolding strategy that enhances student learning and engagement. By providing clear, step-by-step examples, teachers can help students understand complex concepts, acquire new skills, and build confidence in their abilities. Whether in mathematics, literacy, science, history, or art, effective demonstrations can make a significant difference in students' educational experiences. Through careful planning, clear explanations, and interactive elements, teachers can use demonstrations to support and guide their students towards academic success.

BENEFITS OF MODELLING FOR STUDENT UNDERSTANDING

Introduction to the Benefits of Modelling

Modelling is an instructional strategy that significantly enhances student understanding by providing clear, concrete examples of how to perform tasks and apply concepts. By observing the teacher's demonstrations and thought processes, students gain insight into effective strategies and methodologies. This section explores the various benefits of modelling for student comprehension, engagement, confidence, and overall learning outcomes.

Enhancing Comprehension

Modelling makes abstract concepts and complex processes more accessible to students by providing tangible examples. When teachers model a task, they break it down into manageable steps, making it easier for students to follow and understand. This step-by-step approach helps students see the logical sequence and relationships between different components of the task.

For instance, in mathematics, modelling the process of solving a quadratic equation allows students to see each step—from factoring the equation to applying the quadratic formula—thus demystifying the problem-solving process. In literacy, modelling how to analyse a text or write an essay helps students understand the structure and components of these tasks.

According to Rosenshine's Principles of Instruction, effective modelling involves providing students with clear, detailed explanations and examples. This clarity helps students build a solid foundation of understanding, which they can then apply independently (Rosenshine, 2012).

Increasing Engagement

Modelling captures students 'attention and maintains their interest, making the learning experience more engaging. When students watch a live demonstration, they are more likely to stay focused and participate actively in the lesson. This increased engagement is particularly important for kinaesthetic learners, who benefit from seeing and doing rather than just listening or reading.

Interactive elements in modelling, such as asking questions and inviting predictions, further enhance engagement.

Building Confidence

Seeing a task successfully completed by the teacher can significantly boost students' confidence. When students understand what is expected of them and how to achieve it, they are more likely to feel capable and motivated to tackle similar tasks independently. This confidence is crucial for fostering a positive learning environment where students are willing to take risks and make mistakes as part of the learning process.

In a study on the impact of modelling in education, Hattie (2009) found that modelling not only improves students' understanding but also their self-efficacy and motivation. When students feel confident in their abilities, they are more likely to engage in challenging tasks and persist in the face of difficulties.

Supporting Differentiated Instruction

Modelling caters to various learning styles, making it an effective strategy for differentiated instruction. Visual learners benefit from seeing the process, auditory learners from hearing the explanations, and kinaesthetic learners from engaging in the activity. This inclusivity ensures that all students have the opportunity to understand and succeed, regardless of their preferred learning style.

For example, in an art class, a teacher might model a painting technique, showing the steps visually while explaining the process verbally. Students can then practice the technique themselves, receiving immediate feedback and guidance. This multi-modal approach addresses the diverse needs of students and supports more effective learning.

Fostering Independent Learning

One of the key goals of scaffolding is to gradually transfer responsibility from the teacher to the students, fostering independent learning. Modelling plays a crucial role in this process by providing students with the tools and strategies they need to succeed on their own. By observing and practising these strategies, students develop the skills and confidence to apply them independently.

In literacy, for instance, modelling how to annotate a text or organise an essay teaches students specific techniques they can use in their independent work. Over time, students internalise these strategies and become more self-sufficient learners.

Promoting Deep Learning

Modelling encourages deep learning by helping students understand the underlying principles and processes involved in a task. Rather than simply memorising procedures, students learn to think critically and apply their knowledge in different contexts. This deeper understanding is essential for long-term retention and transfer of learning.

In history, for example, modelling how to analyse primary source documents helps students develop critical thinking skills and understand the complexities of historical inquiry. This deeper engagement with the material fosters a more profound and lasting understanding of the subject.

Examples of Effective Modelling in Different Subjects

- Mathematics: Modelling the process of solving algebraic equations, using manipulatives to illustrate fractions and demonstrate geometric concepts.

- Literacy: Demonstrating how to plan and write an essay, using think-aloud strategies to analyse a text and infer meanings.

- Science: Conducting a scientific experiment and explaining each step, demonstrating how to write a lab report and interpret data.

- History: Analysing primary source documents, demonstrating how to construct a timeline and critically evaluate historical evidence.

- Art: Demonstrating painting techniques, showing the process of sketching before painting, and explaining different artistic styles.

Modelling is a powerful and versatile scaffolding strategy that offers numerous benefits for student understanding. By providing clear examples and articulating thought processes, teachers can enhance comprehension, increase engagement, build confidence, support differentiated instruction, foster independent learning, and promote deep learning. When effectively implemented, modelling can transform the educational experience, helping students develop the skills and confidence they need to succeed.

EXAMPLES OF EFFECTIVE MODELLING IN DIFFERENT SUBJECTS

Topic: Making an Omelette

Overview: In this case study, a secondary school design technology (food) teacher models the process of making an omelette using an overhead camera to project the demonstration. The objective is to help students understand each step of the cooking process, learn essential culinary skills, and follow along in real-time to make their own omelettes.

Procedure:

1. Introduction:

    - The teacher begins by introducing the lesson and explaining the objectives: to learn how to make a basic omelette, understand safe food handling practices, and develop cooking skills.

    - The teacher discusses the importance of following instructions carefully and maintaining a clean and organised workspace.

2. Preparation:

    - The teacher displays the list of ingredients and equipment needed for making an omelette on the overhead projector: eggs, milk, salt, pepper, butter, cheese, vegetables (optional), frying pan, whisk, bowl, spatula, and chopping board.

    - The teacher ensures that each student has the necessary ingredients and equipment at their workstation.

Ingredients:

- 2 eggs

- 1 tablespoon of milk

- A pinch of salt

- A pinch of pepper

- 1 tablespoon of butter

- 1/4 cup of grated cheese

- Optional: chopped vegetables (e.g., bell peppers, onions, tomatoes)

Equipment:

- Frying pan

- Whisk

- Mixing bowl

- Spatula

- Chopping board

- Knife

3. Demonstration:
   Using the overhead camera, the teacher models each step of the omelette-making process, providing clear verbal explanations and visual guidance. Students follow along at their workstations.

Step 1: Cracking and Whisking Eggs

- The teacher demonstrates how to crack two eggs into a mixing bowl, ensuring no shell fragments fall in.

- They add one tablespoon of milk, a pinch of salt, and a pinch of pepper to the bowl.

- Using a whisk, the teacher beats the eggs until they are well combined and slightly frothy, explaining the importance of incorporating air for a light and fluffy omelette.

- Students follow along, cracking and whisking their eggs.

Step 2: Preparing the Pan

- The teacher places a frying pan on medium heat and adds one tablespoon of butter, showing how to melt it evenly without burning.

- They explain the importance of a non-stick pan and properly melted butter to prevent sticking.

- Students follow along, preparing their pans and melting the butter.

Step 3: Cooking the Omelette

- The teacher pours the whisked eggs into the pan, tilting it to spread the mixture evenly.

- They explain the technique of gently pushing the edges of the omelette towards the centre with a spatula, allowing the uncooked egg to flow to the edges.

- The teacher demonstrates when and how to add cheese and optional vegetables evenly over the surface.

- Students follow along, cooking their omelettes and adding fillings.

Step 4: Folding and Serving

- Once the omelette is mostly set but still slightly runny on top, the teacher demonstrates how to fold it in half using the spatula.

- They explain the importance of not overcooking the omelette to keep it tender.

- The teacher slides the folded omelette onto a plate, presenting it neatly.

- Students follow along, folding and serving their omelettes.

4. Student Practice:

- Students make their omelettes step-by-step, following the teacher's demonstration.

- The teacher circulates around the room, providing individual feedback and assistance as needed, ensuring students are following safe food handling practices and cooking techniques correctly.

5. Reflection and Discussion:

- Once all students have completed their omelettes, the teacher leads a reflection session.

- Students taste their omelettes and discuss the cooking process, sharing what they found challenging and what they enjoyed.

- The teacher highlights key points from the lesson, such as the importance of preparation, the techniques used, and how these skills can be applied to other cooking tasks.

Resources:

- Worksheet: Includes a list of ingredients and equipment, step-by-step instructions with checkboxes for each step, and a section for students to write reflections and notes.

- Visual Aids: Overhead camera setup to project the teacher's demonstration onto a screen, allowing all students to see the process clearly.

- Safety and Hygiene Guidelines: A handout with essential food safety and hygiene practices to follow in the kitchen.

Topic: Writing a Persuasive Essay

Overview: In this case study, a secondary school English teacher models the process of planning and writing a persuasive essay. The goal is to help students understand how to structure their essay, develop their arguments, and use persuasive language effectively.

Procedure:

1. Introduction: The teacher introduces the topic of the persuasive essay: "Should school uniforms be mandatory?" They discuss the importance of having a clear thesis statement and supporting arguments.

2. Demonstration:

    *   Brainstorming: The teacher models brainstorming by listing potential arguments for and against school uniforms on the board. They encourage students to contribute ideas.

    *   Thesis Statement: The teacher writes a sample thesis statement: "School uniforms should be mandatory because they promote equality, reduce bullying, and save money for families."

    *   Outline: The teacher creates an outline for the essay on the board, including an introduction, three body paragraphs, and a conclusion.

        ◦   Introduction: Hook, background information, thesis statement.

        ◦   Body Paragraph 1: Argument 1 (promote equality) with supporting evidence.

        ◦   Body Paragraph 2: Argument 2 (reduce bullying) with supporting evidence.

        ◦   Body Paragraph 3: Argument 3 (save money) with supporting evidence.

        ◦   Conclusion: Restate thesis, summarise arguments, call to action.

3. Writing: The teacher writes the introduction paragraph in real-time, using a think-aloud strategy to explain their choices: "I'm starting with a hook to grab the reader's attention: 'Imagine a school where every student feels equal and included.' Then, I provide some background information on the debate about school uniforms. Finally, I state my thesis clearly."

4. Student Practice: The teacher provides a worksheet with sentence starters and a graphic organiser to help students plan their essays. Students work on writing their introduction paragraphs and receive feedback from the teacher.

Resources: Worksheet with brainstorming space, sentence starters, and a graphic organiser for essay planning.

Topic: Conducting a Scientific Experiment

Overview: In this case study, a secondary school science teacher models the process of conducting a scientific experiment. The objective is to help students understand the scientific method and how to apply it in a laboratory setting.

Procedure:

1. Introduction: The teacher introduces the experiment: "Investigating the effect of different fertilisers on plant growth." They review the steps of the scientific method: question, hypothesis, experiment, observation, analysis, and conclusion.

2. Demonstration:

   - Question and Hypothesis: The teacher formulates a question: "How do different types of fertilisers affect plant growth?" They then state a hypothesis: "If plants are given organic fertiliser, then they will grow taller than plants given chemical fertiliser."

   - Experiment Setup: The teacher sets up the experiment by planting seeds in three pots: one with organic fertiliser, one with chemical fertiliser, and one without fertiliser (control). They explain each step, from measuring soil and planting seeds to labelling the pots.

   - Observation: The teacher demonstrates how to observe and record data, such as measuring plant height every week. They show how to use a data table to organise observations.

   - Analysis: The teacher models analysing the data by creating a graph to compare the growth of plants in each pot. They discuss patterns and draw conclusions based on the data.

3. Student Practice: Students are provided with their own materials to replicate the experiment in small groups. They use a worksheet to record their hypothesis, observations, and analysis. The teacher circulates to provide guidance and answer questions.

4. Reflection: The teacher leads a class discussion where students share their results and reflect on the scientific process. They compare their findings and discuss any variations or unexpected outcomes.

Resources: Worksheet with sections for hypothesis, data table for observations, and graphing space for analysis.

Topic: Analysing Primary Source Documents

Overview: In this case study, a secondary school history teacher models the process of analysing primary source documents to help students develop critical thinking and historical inquiry skills.

Procedure:

1. Introduction: The teacher introduces a primary source document: a letter from a World War I soldier. They discuss the importance of primary sources in understanding historical events and perspectives.

2. Demonstration:

   - Contextualisation: The teacher provides background information about World War I and the author of the letter. They explain the historical context and significance of the document.

   - Close Reading: The teacher reads the letter aloud, pausing to think aloud about the content: "Here, the soldier describes the conditions in the trenches. I'm noticing the vivid language he uses to convey the harsh realities of war."

   - Questioning: The teacher models asking critical questions: "What does this letter reveal about the soldier's experiences? How does it compare to other accounts of the war?"

   - Corroboration: The teacher compares the letter with another primary source, such as a diary entry from a nurse. They discuss similarities and differences, teaching students how to corroborate evidence.

3. Student Practice: Students work in pairs to analyse a different primary source document. They use a worksheet with guided questions to help them contextualise, close read, question, and corroborate the document.

4. Reflection: The teacher leads a class discussion where students share their analyses and discuss the insights they gained from the primary sources. They reflect on the value of using primary sources in historical research.

Resources: Worksheet with sections for contextualisation, close reading notes, guided questions, and space for corroboration.

Topic: Learning a Painting Technique

Overview: In this case study, an art teacher models a specific painting technique to help students understand the steps involved and develop their own artistic skills.

Procedure:

1. Introduction: The teacher introduces the painting technique: blending colours to create a gradient effect. They explain the importance of this technique in creating realistic and visually appealing artwork.

2. Demonstration:

   - Materials: The teacher shows the materials needed: paint, brushes, canvas, and palette. They explain the purpose of each tool.

   - Technique: The teacher demonstrates the technique step-by-step, explaining each action: "First, I apply a base colour to the canvas. Then, I gradually add a second colour and blend it into the first using smooth, horizontal strokes."

   - Tips and Tricks: The teacher shares tips for achieving a smooth gradient: "It's important to work quickly before the paint dries. Use a clean brush to blend the colours seamlessly."

3. Student Practice: Students receive their own materials to practice the technique. The teacher provides individual feedback and guidance, helping students refine their blending skills.

4. Reflection: The teacher leads a critique session where students display their work and discuss the challenges and successes they experienced. They reflect on the techniques learned and how they can be applied in future projects.

Resources: Checklist for materials, step-by-step instructions for the painting technique, and a reflection worksheet for the critique session.

THINK ALOUD

Think-Aloud Strategies to Show Thought Processes

Think-aloud strategies are a dynamic and effective scaffolding technique that involves the teacher verbalising their thought processes while performing a task. This method provides students with a window into the cognitive strategies and problem-solving approaches used by the teacher, enabling them to internalise and apply these strategies independently. Think-aloud strategies are particularly beneficial for developing metacognitive skills, as they make the often invisible processes of thinking, reasoning, and decision-making explicit and accessible to students.

Implementing Think-Aloud Strategies

To implement think-aloud strategies effectively, teachers should consider the following key practices:

- Select Appropriate Tasks: Choose tasks that naturally lend themselves to cognitive processing and problem-solving. These might include reading comprehension, mathematical problem-solving, scientific inquiry, or writing tasks. The complexity of the task should be suitable for the students' level, challenging them without causing frustration.

- Verbalise Thought Processes: As the teacher performs the task, they should articulate their thinking clearly and comprehensively. This includes making predictions, asking questions, making connections, visualising concepts, and reflecting on decisions. For example, during a reading lesson, a teacher might say, "I predict that the character will face a challenge in the next chapter because of the clues given earlier in the story."

- Model Different Cognitive Strategies: Demonstrate a variety of cognitive strategies, such as summarising, inferencing, questioning, and evaluating. This exposes students to multiple approaches to thinking and problem-solving, which they can adopt and adapt to their own learning.

- Encourage Student Participation: Invite students to participate in the think-aloud process by asking them to share their thoughts, predictions, and questions. This collaborative approach not only engages students but also helps them practise and develop their own metacognitive skills.

- Reflect and Discuss: After the think-aloud session, engage students in a discussion about the strategies used and their effectiveness. This reflection helps reinforce the cognitive processes and allows students to articulate their understanding and insights.

Benefits of Think-Aloud Strategies

Think-aloud strategies offer several significant benefits for student learning:

- Enhanced Metacognition: By modelling their thought processes, teachers help students become more aware of their own thinking. This metacognitive awareness enables students to plan, monitor, and evaluate their learning more effectively.

- Improved Problem-Solving Skills: Think-aloud strategies provide students with concrete examples of how to approach and solve problems. By observing the teacher's reasoning, students learn to apply similar strategies to their own problem-solving tasks.

- Increased Engagement: The interactive nature of think-aloud strategies keeps students engaged and involved in the learning process. It encourages active participation and critical thinking, making learning more dynamic and meaningful.

- Transferable Skills: The cognitive strategies modelled during think-aloud sessions are transferable across different subjects and contexts. Students can apply these strategies to a wide range of tasks, enhancing their overall academic performance.

Examples of Think-Aloud Strategies in Different Subjects

- Literacy: During a reading comprehension lesson, a teacher might read a passage aloud and think aloud about the content. For instance, they might predict what will happen next, question the motives of a character, or make connections to other texts. This helps students develop their own comprehension strategies and enhances their understanding of the text.

- Mathematics: In a mathematics lesson, a teacher might solve a complex problem while verbalising their thought processes. They might explain why they chose a particular method, discuss the steps they are taking, and reflect on the reasonableness of their solution. This modelling helps students understand the problem-solving process and develop their own mathematical reasoning skills.

- Science: During a science experiment, a teacher might think aloud about the scientific method. They might explain their hypothesis, predict the outcome of the experiment, and discuss the results. This helps students understand the scientific inquiry process and develop their own investigative skills.

- History: In a history lesson, a teacher might analyse a primary source document while thinking aloud. They might question the reliability of the source, consider the historical context, and draw inferences about the content. This helps students develop critical thinking and analytical skills, which are essential for historical inquiry.

- Writing: During a writing lesson, a teacher might think aloud while planning and drafting an essay. They might brainstorm ideas, organise their thoughts, and reflect on their word choices. This modelling helps students understand the writing process and develop their own writing skills.

Think-aloud strategies are a powerful tool for scaffolding student learning. By making their cognitive processes visible, teachers provide students with valuable insights into effective thinking and problem-solving strategies. This approach not only enhances students' metacognitive awareness and problem-solving skills but also increases their engagement and confidence in their learning. Through careful implementation and thoughtful reflection, think-aloud strategies can significantly enrich the educational experience and support students' academic growth.

QUESTIONING TECHNIQUES

Introduction to Questioning Techniques

Questioning techniques are pivotal in scaffolding as they drive the learning process by prompting students to think critically, explore new ideas, and engage deeply with the content. Effective questioning not only helps in assessing students' understanding but also encourages active participation and stimulates cognitive development. This section will cover the main types of questions used in scaffolding, strategies for using questions to enhance learning, and methods for encouraging student questions. Additionally, it will delve into Socratic questioning methods and provide practical examples across different subjects.

Types of Questions

Open-ended Questions

Open-ended questions require more than a simple yes or no answer, encouraging students to elaborate, explain, and explore their thoughts. These questions foster deeper thinking and allow students to express their understanding in a comprehensive manner. For example, instead of asking, "Is water a solid at room temperature?" a teacher might ask, "What are the states of water, and how do temperature changes affect these states?"

Probing Questions

Probing questions dig deeper into a student's response, prompting them to expand on their initial answer and think more critically. These questions are useful for uncovering underlying assumptions and encouraging students to reflect further. For example, if a student explains a historical event, a probing question could be, "What were the long-term impacts of this event on society?"

Guiding Questions

Guiding questions are used to steer students towards a particular line of thinking or to help them arrive at conclusions independently. These questions support students in following a logical path of inquiry. For instance, in a science class, a teacher might ask, "What do you predict will happen if we increase the amount of sunlight a plant receives?" followed by, "How can we test this prediction?"

Using Questions to Stimulate Thinking and Learning

Encouraging Critical Thinking

Effective questioning promotes critical thinking by challenging students to analyse, evaluate, and synthesise information. Questions that require students to justify their reasoning or compare and contrast concepts deepen their understanding. For example, in a literature class, a teacher might ask, "How does the protagonist's journey in this novel compare to that of the hero in classical mythology?"

Promoting Active Participation

Incorporating questions throughout a lesson keeps students engaged and actively involved in the learning process. Regular questioning ensures that students are continually processing information and articulating their thoughts. During a classroom discussion, a teacher might use a series of questions to ensure all students contribute and stay involved.

Assessing Understanding

Questions are a powerful tool for formative assessment, helping teachers gauge student comprehension and identify areas needing further clarification. Asking questions like, "Can you explain this concept in your own words?" or "What steps did you take to solve this problem?" provides insight into students' understanding and thought processes.

Socratic Questioning Methods

Socratic questioning is a disciplined questioning technique that promotes deep thinking and illuminates ideas by challenging assumptions and exploring underlying beliefs. This method involves asking a series of thoughtful, open-ended questions to delve into complex topics.

Clarification Questions

These questions help clarify concepts and ideas. For example, "What do you mean by...?" and "Can you give me an example of...?"

Probing Assumptions

These questions challenge the assumptions behind a student's statement. For example, "What are you assuming?" and "How did you come to that assumption?"

Exploring Implications

These questions consider the consequences of an idea or action. For example, "What are the implications of...?" and "How does this affect...?"

Encouraging Student Questions

Encouraging students to ask their own questions fosters curiosity and deeper engagement with the material. Strategies for promoting student questions include:

Creating a Safe Environment

Establishing a classroom culture where all questions are valued and students feel safe to express their thoughts without fear of judgement is crucial.

Using Question Prompts

Providing question stems or prompts helps students formulate their questions. Examples include, "I wonder why...," "What if...," and "How does...?"

Modelling Questioning

Demonstrating effective questioning techniques by regularly posing thoughtful questions during lessons shows students how to ask meaningful questions.

Examples of Questioning Techniques in Different Subjects

Mathematics

In a mathematics class, questioning can guide students through problem-solving processes. For example, "What do we know about this problem?" followed by, "What strategies can we use to solve it?" and "How can we check our solution?"

Literacy

During a reading comprehension lesson, a teacher could ask, "What is the main idea of this paragraph?" and "How do the details support the main idea?" to help students understand the text.

Science

In a science lesson, a teacher might ask, "What hypothesis can we form based on our observations?" and "What evidence supports our hypothesis?" to encourage scientific thinking.

History

In a history class, a teacher might use questions like, "What were the causes of this event?" and "What were its effects?" to help students analyse historical events.

Art

In an art class, a teacher could ask, "What techniques did the artist use in this piece?" and "How do these techniques contribute to the overall effect?" to deepen students' appreciation and understanding of art.

Questioning techniques are vital for promoting student thinking, engagement, and understanding within the framework of scaffolding. By using a variety of question types and strategies, teachers can stimulate deeper learning and foster critical thinking skills. Socratic questioning, in particular, encourages students to explore ideas in depth and develop their analytical abilities. Encouraging student questions further enhances the learning experience, making education a more interactive and dynamic process.

USING GRAPHIC ORGANISERS

Introduction to Graphic Organisers

Graphic organisers are visual tools that help students structure information, making complex concepts more accessible and understandable. They are an effective scaffolding strategy because they provide a visual representation of relationships between ideas, aiding in comprehension and retention. This section will explore various types of graphic organisers, their benefits for visual learners, how to create and implement them in lessons, and provide subject-specific examples.

Types of Graphic Organisers

Mind Maps

Mind maps are diagrams that represent ideas branching out from a central concept. They are useful for brainstorming, organising thoughts, and showing connections between ideas. For example, in a literature class, a mind map can be used to explore the themes and characters of a novel.

Venn Diagrams

Venn diagrams consist of overlapping circles, each representing a set. The overlapping areas show commonalities between the sets, while the non-overlapping areas show differences. Venn diagrams are particularly useful for comparing and contrasting ideas, such as comparing two historical events or scientific processes.

Flowcharts

Flowcharts illustrate the steps in a process or sequence, making them ideal for subjects that involve procedures or algorithms, such as science experiments or mathematical problem-solving. Each step is represented by a box, with arrows indicating the flow from one step to the next.

KWL Charts

KWL charts are divided into three columns: "What I Know," "What I Want to Know," and "What I Learned." These charts help students organise their prior knowledge, set learning goals, and reflect on what they have learned. They are particularly useful at the beginning and end of a unit.

Concept Maps

Concept maps are hierarchical diagrams that show the relationships between different concepts. They start with a main idea at the top and branch out into subtopics. Concept maps are useful for organising complex information, such as the structure of an ecosystem or the causes of a historical event.

Benefits for Visual Learners

Graphic organisers are especially beneficial for visual learners, who understand and retain information better when it is presented visually. These tools enhance comprehension by helping students visualise relationships between ideas, making complex concepts easier to understand. Additionally, visual representations aid in memory retention by organising information in a way that is easy to recall. The process of creating and using graphic organisers can also make learning more interactive and enjoyable, fostering greater student engagement. Furthermore, graphic organisers can be adapted to meet the needs of diverse learners, providing support for those who struggle with traditional text-based instruction.

Creating and Implementing Graphic Organisers in Lessons

Identify the Objective

Determine the purpose of the graphic organiser and what you want students to achieve. This will help you choose the most appropriate type of organiser for your lesson.

Introduce the Organiser

Explain the purpose of the graphic organiser and demonstrate how to use it. Provide a clear example to illustrate its structure and function, ensuring that students understand its relevance to the lesson.

Model the Process

Walk students through the process of filling out the organiser, using a relevant example. Think aloud as you do this, explaining your thought process and how you are organising the information. This step is crucial for showing students how to effectively use the organiser.

Guided Practice

Allow students to practice using the graphic organiser with guidance. Provide feedback and support as they work through the process, helping them to correctly structure and organise their information.

Independent Practice

Once students are comfortable with the organiser, have them use it independently to organise information related to a new topic or task. This encourages them to apply what they have learned and reinforces their understanding.

Review and Reflect

After completing the organiser, review it with the students. Discuss how it helped them understand the material and what they learned from the process. This reflection helps to consolidate their learning and reinforces the value of the organiser.

Examples of Subject-Specific Graphic Organisers

Mathematics

In mathematics, flowcharts can be used to illustrate the steps in solving equations, while Venn diagrams can help compare and contrast different sets or properties. For instance, a flowchart can guide students through the process of solving a quadratic equation step-by-step, helping them understand each stage of the problem-solving process.

Literacy

In literacy, mind maps can help students brainstorm ideas for writing assignments, and KWL charts can be used to organise knowledge before and after reading a text. For example, a mind map can be used to outline the main themes and characters in a novel, helping students to organise their thoughts and ideas coherently.

Science

In science, concept maps can help students understand the relationships between different scientific concepts, while flowcharts can illustrate the steps in an experimental procedure. For instance, a concept map can show the hierarchy and interactions within an ecosystem, making it easier for students to grasp the complexity of ecological relationships.

History

In history, timelines can be used to visualise the sequence of events, while Venn diagrams can compare and contrast different historical periods or figures. For example, a timeline can illustrate the major events leading up to and following the American Revolution, helping students to understand the chronological flow and causality of historical events.

In art, mind maps can help students plan their projects, and concept maps can show the relationships between different artistic styles and movements. For instance, a concept map can illustrate the influences and characteristics of Impressionism, aiding students in understanding the development and impact of the art movement.

Graphic organisers are versatile tools that support scaffolding by helping students visualise and organise information. They are particularly beneficial for visual learners and can be adapted to suit a variety of subjects and learning objectives. By incorporating graphic organisers into lessons, teachers can enhance student comprehension, retention, and engagement, making complex concepts more accessible and understandable.

STEP-BY-STEP INSTRUCTIONS

Introduction to Step-by-Step Instructions

Step-by-step instructions are a fundamental scaffolding strategy that involves breaking down complex tasks into manageable steps. This method provides clear and concise guidance, helping students to understand and accomplish tasks systematically. By structuring tasks into smaller, sequential steps, teachers can reduce student anxiety, improve comprehension, and promote independent learning. This section will explore the importance of step-by-step instructions, methods for providing effective instructions, and examples across different subjects.

Importance of Step-by-Step Instructions

Step-by-step instructions are crucial for helping students navigate complex tasks and concepts. This method aligns with the principles of cognitive load theory, which suggests that breaking information into smaller chunks makes it easier for students to process and understand. By providing clear and structured guidance, teachers can help students build confidence and develop the skills needed to tackle challenging tasks independently.

Methods for Providing Effective Step-by-Step Instructions

> ### Break Down the Task

Divide the task into smaller, manageable steps. Each step should be clear and concise, focusing on one specific part of the task. For example, when teaching how to write an essay, break down the process into steps such as brainstorming ideas, creating an outline, writing a thesis statement, drafting paragraphs, and revising the final draft.

> ### Use Clear and Concise Language

Use simple and direct language to explain each step. Avoid using jargon or overly complex terms that might confuse students. Ensure that the instructions are easy to follow and understand.

Provide Visual Aids

Use visual aids such as diagrams, charts, and checklists to complement the instructions. Visual aids can help students visualise the steps and understand the process better. For example, a flowchart can illustrate the steps involved in solving a math problem.

Demonstrate Each Step

Model the process by demonstrating each step in front of the students. Think aloud as you demonstrate, explaining your thought process and the rationale behind each step. This approach helps students see how to apply the instructions in practice.

Use Checklists and Outlines

Provide students with checklists and outlines to help them keep track of their progress. Checklists can be used to tick off each step as it is completed, ensuring that students follow the sequence correctly.

Encourage Practice and Repetition

Allow students to practice the steps multiple times to reinforce their understanding. Provide feedback and support as they work through the process, helping them to refine their skills and build confidence.

Examples of Step-by-Step Instructions in Various Subjects

Mathematics

In mathematics, step-by-step instructions are essential for solving complex problems. For example, when teaching students how to solve a quadratic equation, the steps might include:

1. Write the equation in standard form.

2. Identify the coefficients (a, b, and c).

3. Apply the quadratic formula.

4. Simplify the solution.

5. Check the solution by substituting it back into the original equation.

Literacy

In literacy, step-by-step instructions can guide students through the writing process. For instance, when writing a persuasive essay, the steps might include:

1. Choose a topic.

2. Conduct research to gather evidence.

3. Create an outline.

4. Write the introduction with a thesis statement.

5. Develop body paragraphs with supporting arguments.

6. Write a conclusion that summarises the main points.

7. Revise and edit the essay for clarity and correctness.

Science

In science, step-by-step instructions are crucial for conducting experiments. For example, when performing a simple chemical reaction experiment, the steps might include:

1. Gather and organise the necessary materials.

2. Measure the required amounts of each chemical.

3. Mix the chemicals in a specific order.

4. Observe and record the reaction.

5. Analyse the results and draw conclusions.

History

In history, step-by-step instructions can help students analyse primary source documents. The steps might include:

1. Identify the type of document and its author.

2. Determine the historical context.

3. Analyse the content for key themes and messages.

4. Corroborate the information with other sources.

5. Discuss the significance of the document.

Art

In art, step-by-step instructions can guide students through creating a piece of artwork. For example, when painting a landscape, the steps might include:

1. Choose a reference image or scene.

2. Sketch the basic outline on the canvas.

3. Block in the main shapes and colours.

4. Add details and refine the shapes.

5. Apply finishing touches and highlights.

CUEING AND PROMPTING

Introduction to Cueing and Prompting

Cueing and prompting are essential scaffolding tools that provide students with guidance as they work through learning tasks. While cues and prompts both support student learning, they differ in their level of directness. Cues are subtle hints that encourage students to recall prior knowledge or look for clues, whereas prompts are more direct and specific, guiding students towards particular information or strategies. For example, a cue might be, "Is there anything in the room that could support us?" whereas a prompt might be, "Is there anything on that poster about topic X that will help?"

Types of Cues and Prompts

Verbal Cues

Verbal cues involve giving students spoken hints that gently nudge them towards the solution. These cues are designed to trigger recall or suggest a direction without providing the complete answer. For instance, if a student is struggling to remember a historical date, a teacher might say, "Think about the events that happened around the turn of the century."

Visual Cues

Visual cues include diagrams, illustrations, or highlighted text that help students focus on relevant information or concepts. These can be particularly effective for visual learners. For instance, a teacher might underline key terms in a reading passage or use arrows to highlight important parts of a map.

Written Cues

Written cues are similar to verbal cues but are provided in written form. They can be included in worksheets, margin notes, or on the board. For example, in a science assignment, a teacher might write, "Consider the role of photosynthesis in this process" to guide students' thinking.

Prompts

Prompts are specific questions or statements that directly guide students to think about particular aspects of the task. These prompts are more explicit than cues and often require immediate student response. For example, in a mathematics class, a teacher might ask, "What is the first step in solving this equation?" or "How can you apply the Pythagorean theorem here?"

Benefits of Using Cues and Prompts

Cueing and prompting offer several significant benefits in the learning process:

Encouraging Critical Thinking

By providing just enough guidance to stimulate thought, cues and prompts encourage students to think critically about the problem at hand. This helps them develop reasoning skills and enhances their ability to solve problems independently.

Promoting Independence

Rather than giving students the answers, cues and prompts support them as they work through challenges on their own. This fosters a sense of independence and confidence in their ability to learn and succeed.

Reducing Anxiety

When faced with difficult tasks, students can become anxious or frustrated. Cues and prompts provide reassurance and direction, helping to alleviate anxiety and keep students engaged with the task.

Enhancing Engagement

By making tasks more manageable, cues and prompts keep students engaged and motivated. This sustained engagement is crucial for effective learning and retention of information.

Types of Effective Cues and Prompts in Various Subjects

Mathematics

In mathematics, verbal cues can guide students through problem-solving steps without giving away the solution. For instance, if a student is struggling with a geometry problem, a teacher might say, "Think about the properties of triangles you know." A prompt in the same context might be, "What do we know about the angles in an equilateral triangle?"

Literacy

In literacy, prompts can help students with reading comprehension and writing tasks. For example, a teacher might prompt a student by asking, "What do you think the author is trying to convey in this paragraph?" A cue could be, "Look for the main idea in the first and last sentences."

Science

In science, visual cues such as labelled diagrams can help students understand complex processes. During an experiment, a teacher might use prompts like, "What do you predict will happen if we change this variable?" A cue might be, "Observe the colour change in the solution."

History

In history, written cues can guide students in their analysis of primary sources. For example, a margin note might suggest, "Consider the author's perspective and how it might influence the account." A prompt could be, "How does this document reflect the social attitudes of its time?"

Art

In art, visual and verbal cues can help students understand techniques and concepts. A teacher might use a visual cue by demonstrating a brushstroke technique and then prompt students by asking, "How can you use this technique to create texture in your painting?"

Cueing and prompting are versatile and powerful scaffolding tools that support student learning by providing subtle guidance and encouraging independent problem-solving. By carefully designing and implementing cues and prompts, teachers can enhance critical thinking, reduce anxiety, promote engagement, and foster independence across various subjects. This approach helps students develop the skills and confidence they need to tackle challenges and succeed academically.

USE OF ANALOGIES AND METAPHORS

Introduction to the Use of Analogies and Metaphors

Analogies and metaphors are powerful scaffolding tools that relate new concepts to familiar ones, making abstract or complex ideas more accessible and comprehensible. By drawing parallels between known and unknown concepts, teachers can enhance student understanding, promote retention, and foster deeper learning. This section will explore the benefits of using analogies and metaphors, strategies for effectively incorporating them into lessons, and provide examples across various subjects.

Benefits of Using Analogies and Metaphors

Enhancing Comprehension

Analogies and metaphors simplify complex ideas by linking them to familiar experiences or objects. This connection helps students grasp difficult concepts more easily. For instance, comparing the structure of an atom to a solar system helps students visualise and understand the arrangement of electrons around a nucleus.

Promoting Retention

Relating new information to existing knowledge aids memory retention. Analogies and metaphors create mental images that are easier to recall. For example, describing DNA as a "blueprint" for the body helps students remember its role in genetics.

Encouraging Critical Thinking

Analogies and metaphors stimulate critical thinking by encouraging students to identify similarities and differences between the compared entities. This process helps students deepen their understanding and apply their knowledge to new situations.

Fostering Engagement

Using analogies and metaphors makes learning more engaging and relatable. These tools can capture students' interest and make lessons more enjoyable. For example, explaining economic principles using everyday shopping experiences can make the subject more appealing to students.

Strategies for Effectively Using Analogies and Metaphors

Choose Relevant Analogies

Select analogies that are relevant and familiar to your students' experiences. The more relatable the analogy, the more effective it will be in aiding understanding. Consider your students' background knowledge and interests when choosing analogies.

Explain the Connection

Clearly explain the connection between the analogy and the concept being taught. Highlight the similarities and address any limitations of the analogy to avoid misconceptions. For example, while comparing the heart to a pump is helpful, it's important to explain that the heart has more complex functions than a simple mechanical pump.

Use Visual Aids

Incorporate visual aids to complement your analogies and metaphors. Diagrams, illustrations, and physical models can enhance understanding and retention. For example, using a visual of a tree to explain the structure of an essay can help students better organise their writing.

Encourage Student Analogies

Encourage students to create their own analogies and metaphors. This practice helps them actively engage with the material and deepen their understanding. For example, ask students to come up with their own comparisons for the water cycle.

Review and Reflect

After using an analogy or metaphor, review its effectiveness with the students. Discuss how the analogy helped their understanding and address any remaining questions. This reflection reinforces learning and clarifies any misunderstandings.

Examples of Analogies and Metaphors in Different Subjects

Mathematics

In mathematics, analogies can help explain abstract concepts. For instance, comparing fractions to slices of a pizza helps students understand how fractions represent parts of a whole. Similarly, describing the process of solving an equation as "balancing a scale" helps students grasp the concept of maintaining equality.

Literacy

In literacy, metaphors can enrich students' comprehension and writing skills. For example, comparing a narrative structure to a rollercoaster ride—with its ups, downs, and loops—can help students understand plot development. Additionally, teaching metaphors and similes in poetry enhances students' appreciation and use of figurative language.

Science

In science, analogies and metaphors can simplify complex processes. For example, describing the function of a cell membrane as a "security gate" helps students understand its role in regulating what enters and exits the cell. Comparing the nervous system to a "telephone network" can clarify how signals are transmitted throughout the body.

History

In history, analogies can help students understand historical events and relationships. For instance, comparing the rise and fall of empires to a "lifespan" with birth, growth, peak, and decline phases can make the concept more relatable. Using the metaphor of a "melting pot" to describe cultural assimilation helps students grasp the idea of diverse cultures blending together.

Art

In art, analogies and metaphors can explain artistic techniques and concepts. For example, comparing the use of light and shadow in a painting to "adding depth and dimension" helps students understand how these elements create a three-dimensional effect. Describing the creative process as a "journey" can inspire students to view their artistic development as an evolving adventure.

Analogies and metaphors are invaluable scaffolding tools that enhance comprehension, promote retention, encourage critical thinking, and foster engagement. By effectively incorporating these tools into lessons, teachers can make complex concepts more accessible and relatable, helping students to better understand and retain new information. When used thoughtfully, analogies and metaphors can transform the learning experience, making education more dynamic and impactful.

COLLABORATIVE LEARNING

Introduction to Collaborative Learning

Collaborative learning is a scaffolding strategy that involves students working together in groups to achieve common learning goals. This approach leverages the collective knowledge and skills of the group, promoting deeper understanding through interaction and cooperation. Collaborative learning fosters communication, critical thinking, and problem-solving skills, making it an essential component of effective teaching. This section will explore the benefits of collaborative learning, strategies for structuring group activities, and provide examples of successful collaborative learning strategies across different subjects.

Benefits of Collaborative Learning

> Enhancing Understanding

Collaborative learning allows students to explain concepts to each other, ask questions, and share different perspectives. This peer-to-peer interaction helps deepen understanding and reinforces learning. Students often find it easier to relate to explanations given by their peers, which can clarify difficult concepts.

> Developing Social Skills

Working in groups helps students develop important social skills, such as communication, teamwork, and conflict resolution. These skills are essential for success in both academic and professional settings. Collaborative learning provides opportunities for students to practice these skills in a structured environment.

> Increasing Engagement

Collaborative learning activities are often more engaging than traditional lecture-based instruction. The interactive nature of group work keeps students actively involved and motivated. When students are engaged, they are more likely to participate, contribute, and retain information.

Fostering Critical Thinking

Group discussions and problem-solving activities encourage students to think critically and creatively. Collaborative learning challenges students to consider multiple viewpoints and to justify their reasoning. This process helps them develop higher-order thinking skills.

Promoting Independence

By working together, students learn to rely on each other and themselves, rather than solely on the teacher. This fosters a sense of independence and confidence in their abilities. Collaborative learning empowers students to take ownership of their learning.

Strategies for Structuring Group Activities

Define Clear Objectives

Clearly define the objectives of the group activity and communicate them to the students. Ensure that each student understands what they are expected to achieve by the end of the activity. Clear objectives help keep the group focused and on task.

Create Diverse Groups

Form groups with diverse skill levels, backgrounds, and perspectives. This diversity enriches the learning experience, as students can learn from each other's strengths and insights. Aim for balanced groups where all members can contribute meaningfully.

Assign Roles

Assign specific roles to each group member to ensure active participation and accountability. Roles can include a facilitator, recorder, presenter, and timekeeper. Assigning roles helps distribute responsibilities evenly and ensures that all students are engaged.

Provide Structured Tasks

Design structured tasks that require collaboration and input from all group members. Tasks should be challenging but achievable, encouraging students to work together to find solutions. Provide clear instructions and resources to support the group work.

Monitor and Support

Circulate among the groups to monitor progress, provide guidance, and address any issues that arise. Offer support and feedback as needed, but allow the groups to work independently as much as possible. This balance helps students develop autonomy while ensuring they stay on track.

Reflect and Debrief

After the activity, conduct a debriefing session where groups can share their findings and reflect on the collaborative process. Discuss what worked well, what challenges were encountered, and what could be improved. Reflection helps consolidate learning and provides insights for future activities.

Examples of Successful Collaborative Learning Strategies

Mathematics

In mathematics, collaborative learning can be used for problem-solving activities. For example, students can work in groups to solve complex word problems. Each group member can take on a different role, such as reading the problem, identifying key information, performing calculations, and checking the solution. This approach encourages students to discuss and justify their strategies, deepening their understanding of mathematical concepts.

Literacy

In literacy, collaborative learning can be applied to reading and writing tasks. For instance, students can work in literature circles to discuss a novel. Each student can assume a role, such as summariser, questioner, connector, and predictor. This structure promotes active reading and critical discussion, enhancing comprehension and analytical skills.

Science

In science, collaborative learning can be used for experiments and projects. For example, students can work in groups to design and conduct an experiment. Roles can include hypothesis generator, materials manager, data recorder, and results presenter. Collaborative experimentation fosters scientific inquiry and teamwork.

History

In history, collaborative learning can be used for research and analysis activities. For instance, students can work in groups to investigate a historical event or figure. Each group member can take on a different aspect of the research, such as gathering primary sources, analysing secondary sources, and creating a presentation. This approach encourages critical thinking and a deeper understanding of historical contexts.

Art

In art, collaborative learning can be used for creative projects. For example, students can work in groups to create a mural or sculpture. Roles can include designer, materials coordinator, painter, and quality checker. Collaborative art projects promote creativity, communication, and project management skills.

Collaborative learning is a powerful scaffolding strategy that enhances student understanding, develops social skills, increases engagement, fosters critical thinking, and promotes independence. By structuring group activities effectively and providing appropriate support, teachers can create a dynamic and interactive learning environment. Collaborative learning prepares students for future academic and professional success by equipping them with essential skills and a deeper understanding of the subject matter.

CHAPTER 4: SCAFFOLDING IN PRIMARY SCHOOLS

Scaffolding is a fundamental instructional strategy in primary education, where it serves as a vital tool for supporting young learners as they acquire new skills and knowledge. The concept of scaffolding involves providing temporary support to students, enabling them to perform tasks that they would not be able to accomplish independently. As students gain proficiency, these supports are gradually removed, fostering independence and confidence. In primary schools, scaffolding helps bridge the gap between what students currently know and what they need to learn, making complex concepts more accessible and manageable.

Importance of Scaffolding in Early Learning

The early years of education are critical for laying the foundation of lifelong learning. Scaffolding plays a crucial role during this period by ensuring that students are not overwhelmed by new information and skills. By breaking down learning into manageable steps and providing targeted support, teachers can help young learners build a solid understanding of fundamental concepts. Scaffolding also promotes a positive learning experience, reducing frustration and boosting self-esteem. This supportive environment encourages students to take risks, ask questions, and develop a love for learning.

Adapting Scaffolding Techniques for Young Learners

Adapting scaffolding techniques to suit the developmental stages of young learners is essential for their success. Young children have unique learning needs and abilities, which require specific strategies to effectively scaffold their learning. Techniques such as modelling, think-alouds, and guided practice can be tailored to be age-appropriate and engaging. For example, using simple language, visual aids, and interactive activities can help maintain the interest and attention of young students. Additionally, incorporating frequent feedback and encouragement is important to reinforce learning and build confidence.

Developmental Considerations in Scaffolding

Understanding the developmental stages of primary school students is crucial for effective scaffolding. Young learners are at different cognitive, social, and emotional developmental stages, which influence how they process information and interact with others. Teachers must consider these factors when designing scaffolding strategies. For instance, younger children may require more concrete examples and hands-on activities, while older primary students might benefit from more abstract thinking and problem-solving tasks. Tailoring scaffolding to align with students' developmental levels ensures that support is appropriate and effective.

Role of Play and Exploration in Scaffolding

Play and exploration are integral components of scaffolding in primary education. Through play, children engage in hands-on, experiential learning that allows them to explore concepts in a meaningful and enjoyable way. Teachers can scaffold learning by guiding play activities, asking probing questions, and introducing new challenges that build on what children already know. Exploration fosters curiosity and creativity, encouraging students to experiment and discover new ideas. By integrating play and exploration into scaffolding strategies, teachers can create a dynamic and interactive learning environment that supports cognitive and social development.

Engaging Parents and Caregivers in Scaffolding

Parents and caregivers play a vital role in the scaffolding process, extending learning beyond the classroom. Engaging them in their children's education helps reinforce skills and concepts at home. Teachers can provide parents with strategies and resources to support their children's learning, such as reading together, practising math skills, and encouraging exploration and curiosity. Regular communication between teachers and parents ensures that scaffolding is consistent and aligned with the students' needs. By involving parents and caregivers, the scaffolding process becomes a collaborative effort that enhances the overall learning experience.

Impact of Scaffolding on Early Academic Success

The impact of scaffolding on early academic success is profound. Research has shown that effective scaffolding can significantly improve students' academic outcomes, including literacy, numeracy, and social-emotional skills. Scaffolding helps build a strong foundation for future learning by ensuring that students master essential skills and concepts early on. Additionally, the confidence and independence gained through scaffolding prepare students for more complex and challenging tasks as they progress in their education. Ultimately, scaffolding sets the stage for a lifelong love of learning and academic achievement.

SCAFFOLDING IN A PRIMARY WRITING LESSON: PRESENTING AN ARGUMENT

Lesson Overview: In this writing lesson, students will learn how to present an argument effectively. The lesson will focus on structuring an argument, using evidence to support claims, and writing persuasively. The scaffolding techniques will range from minimal to extensive support, with a focus on providing the least help first. This approach allows students to attempt tasks independently before receiving additional support, promoting independence and problem-solving skills. The following sequence of scaffolding tools is designed for a single student, acknowledging that some students may need only one type of support, while others may require a combination of techniques.

Lesson Goal: Students will write a persuasive paragraph presenting an argument on a given topic, such as "Should school uniforms be mandatory?"

> ## Scaffolding Tools and Sequence

1. **Cueing and Prompting (Least Support)**

   - Purpose: To provide subtle guidance that encourages students to think independently.

   - Method: Use verbal or written cues and prompts to guide students as they write. These can be questions or statements that remind students of what to include next.

   - Example: "What is your main reason for supporting school uniforms? Can you think of an example to support that reason?"

   - TA/LSA Support: A Teaching Assistant (TA) or Learning Support Assistant (LSA) can circulate the room, providing cues and prompts to students who need a gentle nudge to get started or to keep on track.

2. **Graphic Organisers**

   - Purpose: To help students organise their ideas visually before writing.

   - Method: Provide students with a graphic organiser, such as a mind map or a structured outline. This helps them plan their argument, including the main point, supporting reasons, and evidence.

- Example: The organiser includes sections for the topic sentence, three reasons with supporting evidence, and a concluding statement. Students fill out each section with guidance from the teacher.
- TA/LSA Support: The TA/LSA can assist students in filling out their graphic organisers, ensuring they have clear and organised ideas before they begin writing.

3. Step-by-Step Instructions

- Purpose: To break down the writing task into manageable steps.
- Method: The teacher provides a checklist or set of instructions that outline each part of the paragraph. Students follow these steps to ensure they include all necessary components.
- Example: "Step 1: Write your topic sentence. Step 2: List your first reason and support it with evidence. Step 3: List your second reason and support it with evidence. Step 4: List your third reason and support it with evidence. Step 5: Write a concluding statement."
- TA/LSA Support: The TA/LSA can help students follow the checklist, providing support and clarification as needed.

4. Modelling

- Purpose: To provide students with a clear example of how to write a persuasive paragraph.
- Method: The teacher writes a sample paragraph on the board, thinking aloud to explain each step. This includes brainstorming reasons, structuring the paragraph with a clear topic sentence, supporting evidence, and a concluding statement.
- Example: "Let's brainstorm reasons why school uniforms should be mandatory. One reason is that they promote equality among students. I'll write a topic sentence: 'School uniforms should be mandatory because they promote equality among students.' Now, I'll provide evidence: 'When students wear the same clothes, it reduces the pressure to wear expensive or fashionable items, making everyone feel included.' Finally, I'll conclude: 'Therefore, school uniforms create a more inclusive school environment.'"

- TA/LSA Support: While the teacher models the writing process, the TA/LSA can circulate and provide additional explanations to students who may still be confused.

5. Think-Aloud Strategies (Most Support)

- Purpose: To verbalise the thought process involved in writing an argument.

- Method: The teacher continues to model writing while explicitly stating their thinking. This includes discussing how to choose the strongest evidence and how to link ideas coherently.

- Example: "I'm choosing this evidence because it's something all students can relate to. I'll make sure to connect it back to my main point by using phrases like 'this shows' and 'therefore.'"

- TA/LSA Support: The TA/LSA can work with individual students or small groups, using think-aloud strategies to help them articulate their thought processes and understand the teacher's model.

This sequence acknowledges the principle of "least help first" by starting with minimal support and gradually providing more extensive scaffolding as needed. By tailoring the level of support to individual students, teachers can promote independence and confidence while ensuring that all students have the tools they need to succeed. The TA/LSA plays a crucial role in providing additional support, particularly with graphic organisers, step-by-step instructions, and reinforcing the teacher's modelling and think-aloud strategies.

SCAFFOLDING IN A PRIMARY MATH LESSON: UNDERSTANDING FRACTIONS

Lesson Overview: In this math lesson, students will learn how to understand and work with fractions. The lesson will focus on identifying fractions, understanding equivalent fractions, and comparing fractions. The scaffolding techniques will range from minimal to extensive support, with a focus on providing the least help first. This approach allows students to attempt tasks independently before receiving additional support, promoting independence and problem-solving skills.

Lesson Goal: Students will be able to identify, compare, and understand equivalent fractions.

Scaffolding Tools and Sequence

1. Cueing and Prompting (Least Support)

   - Purpose: To provide subtle guidance that encourages students to think independently.

   - Method: Use verbal or written cues and prompts to guide students as they work with fractions. These can be questions or statements that remind students of key concepts.

   - Example: "What do you notice about the size of the pieces in these two fractions?" or "Can you find another way to show this fraction?"

   - TA/LSA Support: The TA/LSA can circulate the room, providing cues and prompts to students who need a gentle nudge to get started or to keep on track.

2. Manipulatives and Visual Aids

   - Purpose: To provide concrete representations of fractions to enhance understanding.

   - Method: Use fraction circles, bars, or other manipulatives to help students visualise fractions. Visual aids such as fraction charts can also support learning.

- Example: Give students fraction circles to compare the sizes of different fractions physically. Use a fraction chart to show equivalent fractions visually.

- TA/LSA Support: The TA/LSA can assist students in using manipulatives and understanding visual aids, ensuring they grasp the concepts.

3. Graphic Organisers

- Purpose: To help students organise their understanding of fractions visually.

- Method: Provide students with a graphic organiser, such as a fraction chart or a number line. This helps them compare fractions and understand equivalency.

- Example: Use a number line to place fractions in order, helping students see the relationship between different fractions.

- TA/LSA Support: The TA/LSA can help students fill out their graphic organisers, ensuring they have a clear visual representation of the fractions.

4. Step-by-Step Instructions

- Purpose: To break down the task of comparing and finding equivalent fractions into manageable steps.

- Method: Provide a checklist or set of instructions that outline each part of the process. Students follow these steps to ensure they understand each component.

- Example: "Step 1: Identify the fractions you are comparing. Step 2: Use fraction circles to visualise the fractions. Step 3: Place the fractions on a number line. Step 4: Determine if the fractions are equivalent."

- TA/LSA Support: The TA/LSA can help students follow the checklist, providing support and clarification as needed.

5. Interactive Games and Activities

- Purpose: To reinforce understanding through engaging and interactive practice.

- Method: Use games and activities that focus on fractions. These can include online fraction games, card games, or interactive whiteboard activities.

- Example: A fraction matching game where students match equivalent fractions, or an online game where students place fractions on a number line.
- TA/LSA Support: The TA/LSA can facilitate these activities, ensuring students stay engaged and understand the concepts being practiced.

6. Modelling

- Purpose: To provide students with a clear example of how to compare and find equivalent fractions.
- Method: The teacher demonstrates how to compare fractions and find equivalents using manipulatives and visual aids. This includes explaining each step clearly.
- Example: "Let's compare 1/2 and 1/4 using fraction circles. See how two 1/4 pieces fit into one 1/2 piece? This shows that 1/2 is equivalent to 2/4."
- TA/LSA Support: While the teacher models the process, the TA/LSA can circulate and provide additional explanations to students who may still be confused.

7. Think-Aloud Strategies (Most Support)

- Purpose: To verbalise the thought process involved in understanding fractions.
- Method: The teacher continues to model the process while explicitly stating their thinking. This includes discussing how to determine equivalency and compare fractions.
- Example: "I'm noticing that when I divide the fraction circle into more pieces, each piece gets smaller. So, 1/3 is larger than 1/4 because it is divided into fewer pieces."
- TA/LSA Support: The TA/LSA can work with individual students or small groups, using think-aloud strategies to help them articulate their thought processes and understand the teacher's model.

This sequence acknowledges the principle of "least help first" by starting with minimal support and gradually providing more extensive scaffolding as needed. By tailoring the level of support to individual students, teachers can promote independence and confidence while ensuring that all students have the tools they need to succeed. The

TA/LSA plays a crucial role in providing additional support, particularly with manipulatives, graphic organisers, and reinforcing the teacher's modelling and think-aloud strategies. Interactive games and activities provide an engaging way for students to practice and reinforce their understanding of fractions.

CHAPTER 5: SCAFFOLDING IN SECONDARY SCHOOLS AND FURTHER EDUCATION

Scaffolding remains an essential instructional strategy in secondary education, supporting students as they encounter more complex and demanding academic content. At this stage, scaffolding involves not only providing temporary support but also encouraging students to develop self-regulation and independent learning skills. The aim is to guide students through challenging tasks while gradually increasing their autonomy, enabling them to become confident, self-sufficient learners.

Importance of Scaffolding in Adolescent Learning

Adolescence is a critical period for cognitive, emotional, and social development. Effective scaffolding during these years helps students manage the increased academic demands and social pressures they face. By providing structured support and gradually reducing it, teachers can help students develop resilience, problem-solving abilities, and a positive attitude towards learning, all of which are crucial for their success both in school and beyond.

Adapting Scaffolding Techniques for Older Students
Adapting scaffolding techniques for older students involves recognising their growing need for independence and self-regulation. Techniques such as peer collaboration, self-assessment, and technology integration can be particularly effective. Teachers can gradually reduce support as students become more proficient, encouraging them to take greater responsibility for their learning. This section will discuss how to tailor scaffolding strategies to meet the developmental needs of adolescents, fostering autonomy while providing necessary guidance.

Developmental Considerations in Scaffolding for Teenagers
Understanding the developmental stages of teenagers is essential for effective scaffolding. Adolescents are developing advanced cognitive abilities, including abstract thinking, problem-solving, and critical analysis. They are also navigating complex social

dynamics and emotional changes. Teachers must consider these factors when designing scaffolding strategies, ensuring that support is appropriate and responsive to students' developmental needs. This section will explore how to align scaffolding techniques with the cognitive, social, and emotional development of secondary students.

Role of Collaborative Learning and Self-Regulation in Scaffolding

Collaborative learning and self-regulation are key components of scaffolding in secondary education. Group activities, peer tutoring, and collaborative projects provide opportunities for students to learn from each other and develop essential social skills. Self-regulation strategies, such as goal-setting, self-monitoring, and reflective practices, help students take control of their learning and develop independence. This section will discuss how to incorporate collaborative learning and self-regulation into scaffolding strategies, promoting a supportive and interactive learning environment.

Engaging Parents and Caregivers in Secondary Education Scaffolding

Parents and caregivers continue to play a vital role in supporting secondary students' learning. Engaging them in the scaffolding process helps reinforce skills and concepts at home, providing a consistent and supportive learning environment. Teachers can involve parents and caregivers by providing resources, regular communication, and strategies for supporting their children's academic progress. This section will explore how to engage parents and caregivers in scaffolding, enhancing the overall effectiveness of secondary education.

Impact of Scaffolding on Secondary Academic Success

The impact of scaffolding on secondary academic success is profound. Research has shown that effective scaffolding can significantly improve students' academic outcomes, including literacy, numeracy, and scientific reasoning skills. Scaffolding helps build a strong foundation for future learning by ensuring that students master essential skills and concepts early on. Additionally, the confidence and independence gained through scaffolding prepare students for more complex and challenging tasks as they progress in their education. This section will highlight the long-term benefits of scaffolding in secondary education, setting the stage for lifelong academic and career success.

SCAFFOLDING ADVANCED READING COMPREHENSION AND ANALYSIS

In secondary education, students encounter more complex texts that require advanced comprehension and analysis skills. Scaffolding these skills involves providing structured support while encouraging independent critical thinking.

1. Cueing and Prompting:

   - Purpose: To guide students through complex texts by prompting them to consider key ideas and themes.

   - Method: Use open-ended questions and prompts that encourage students to think deeply about the text.

   - Example: "What do you think the author is trying to convey in this passage? Can you find evidence to support your interpretation?"

2. Literature Circles and Socratic Seminars:

   - Purpose: To foster collaborative analysis and discussion of texts.

   - Method: Organise students into small groups (literature circles) or whole-class discussions (Socratic seminars) where they can share their interpretations and ask questions.

   - Example: Assign roles within literature circles (e.g., discussion director, summariser, connector) to structure the discussion and ensure active participation.

3. Graphic Organisers:

   - Purpose: To help students organise their thoughts and analyse text structure and themes.

   - Method: Provide graphic organisers, such as Venn diagrams or plot diagrams, to help students visualise connections and patterns in the text.

   - Example: Use a plot diagram to map out the key events of a story, helping students understand narrative structure.

4. Modelling:

   - Purpose: To demonstrate advanced reading and analysis techniques.

- Method: The teacher reads a passage aloud and models how to annotate the text, identify literary devices, and analyse themes.

- Example: "As I read this paragraph, I'm noticing the use of metaphor. I'll underline it and write a note in the margin about how it contributes to the theme of transformation."

5. Think-Aloud Strategies:

- Purpose: To verbalise the thought process involved in analysing complex texts.

- Method: The teacher thinks aloud while analysing a passage, explaining their reasoning and how they draw conclusions from the text.

- Example: "I'm thinking about why the author chose this particular setting. It seems to symbolise the character's inner conflict."

SCAFFOLDING HIGHER-LEVEL MATH CONCEPTS (ALGEBRA, GEOMETRY, CALCULUS)

Scaffolding in secondary math involves breaking down complex problems into manageable steps and encouraging students to develop problem-solving strategies.

1. Cueing and Prompting:

   - Purpose: To guide students through challenging math problems by asking probing questions.

   - Method: Use prompts to help students identify key steps and strategies.

   - Example: "What is the first step in solving this equation? How can you isolate the variable?"

2. Technology and Visual Aids:

   - Purpose: To enhance understanding through interactive and visual tools.

   - Method: Incorporate graphing calculators, software, and visual aids to illustrate mathematical concepts.

   - Example: Use a graphing calculator to visualise the graph of a quadratic function and explore its properties.

3. Graphic Organisers:

   - Purpose: To help students organise their problem-solving process.

   - Method: Provide graphic organisers, such as flowcharts or problem-solving templates, to structure their approach.

   - Example: Use a flowchart to outline the steps for solving a system of equations.

4. Step-by-Step Instructions:

   - Purpose: To break down complex problems into sequential steps.

   - Method: Provide detailed instructions and checklists to guide students through multi-step problems.

   - Example: "Step 1: Factor the quadratic equation. Step 2: Set each factor equal to zero. Step 3: Solve for the variable."

5. Peer Collaboration:

- Purpose: To promote collaborative problem-solving and peer support.

- Method: Organise students into pairs or small groups to work on challenging problems together.

- Example: Students work in pairs to solve a geometry proof, discussing each step and reasoning through the problem together.

SCAFFOLDING INQUIRY-BASED LEARNING IN SECONDARY SCIENCE

Inquiry-based learning in science encourages students to explore, ask questions, and develop a deeper understanding of scientific concepts through hands-on activities and experiments.

1. Cueing and Prompting:

   - Purpose: To guide students through scientific investigations by asking probing questions.

   - Method: Use prompts to help students formulate hypotheses and design experiments.

   - Example: "What do you think will happen if we change this variable? How can you test your hypothesis?"

2. Lab Experiments and Scientific Investigations:

   - Purpose: To provide hands-on experiences that enhance understanding of scientific concepts.

   - Method: Conduct lab experiments and investigations that require students to apply scientific methods.

   - Example: Students design and conduct an experiment to test the effect of light on plant growth, recording their observations and analysing the results.

3. Graphic Organisers:

   - Purpose: To help students organise their scientific investigations and data.

   - Method: Provide graphic organisers, such as lab report templates or data tables, to structure their work.

   - Example: Use a lab report template to guide students through the process of documenting their experiment, from hypothesis to conclusion.

4. Modelling:

   - Purpose: To demonstrate scientific techniques and methods.

- Method: The teacher models how to conduct an experiment, collect data, and analyse results.

- Example: "Watch as I set up this experiment. I'll explain each step and show you how to record your observations."

5. Think-Aloud Strategies:

- Purpose: To verbalise the thought process involved in scientific inquiry.

- Method: The teacher thinks aloud while designing an experiment, explaining their reasoning and how they draw conclusions from the data.

- Example: "I'm thinking about how to control variables in this experiment. I'll need to keep the amount of water and soil consistent for each plant."

SCAFFOLDING SOCIAL SKILLS AND EMOTIONAL REGULATION FOR ADOLESCENTS

Scaffolding social skills and emotional regulation helps students develop the ability to interact positively with others and manage their emotions effectively.

1. Role-Play and Real-World Scenarios:

   - Purpose: To provide opportunities for students to practice social interactions and problem-solving.

   - Method: Use role-playing activities and real-world scenarios to practice skills such as conflict resolution and empathy.

   - Example: Students role-play a scenario where they must resolve a disagreement with a classmate, discussing their feelings and finding a compromise.

2. Peer Support and Collaboration:

   - Purpose: To promote collaborative learning and peer support.

   - Method: Organise group activities and projects that require students to work together and support each other.

   - Example: Students work in groups to create a presentation on a social issue, developing teamwork and communication skills.

3. Think-Aloud Strategies:

   - Purpose: To model positive social interactions and emotional regulation.

   - Method: The teacher thinks aloud while discussing how to handle a challenging social situation, explaining their thought process and strategies.

   - Example: "If I were in this situation, I would take a deep breath and try to understand the other person's perspective before responding."

4. Graphic Organisers:

   - Purpose: To help students organise their thoughts and strategies for managing emotions.

- Method: Provide graphic organisers, such as emotion charts or conflict resolution templates, to structure their approach.

- Example: Use an emotion chart to help students identify and label their feelings, and a conflict resolution template to plan how to address a disagreement.

5. Reflective Practices:

- Purpose: To encourage self-reflection and personal growth.

- Method: Use reflective practices, such as journaling or group discussions, to help students reflect on their experiences and develop self-awareness.

- Example: Students write in a journal about a recent social interaction, reflecting on what went well and what they could improve.

A NOTE ABOUT FURTHER EDUCATION

Importance of Scaffolding in Further Education (FE)

Scaffolding in further education is essential for supporting young adults as they transition to more independent and self-directed learning environments. Effective scaffolding helps students develop the skills and confidence needed to succeed in vocational training, higher education, and the workforce.

Developmentally Appropriate Scaffolding Techniques for Young Adults

Scaffolding techniques for young adults should focus on promoting autonomy and self-regulation while providing the necessary support to navigate complex tasks and concepts. Techniques such as mentoring, peer collaboration, and the use of technology can be particularly effective.

Role of Independent Study and Self-Directed Learning in Scaffolding

Independent study and self-directed learning are crucial components of scaffolding in further education. Encouraging students to take ownership of their learning and providing them with the tools and strategies to do so fosters independence and lifelong learning skills.

Strategies for Scaffolding Vocational Skills and Career Readiness

1. Mentoring and Coaching:

    - Purpose: To provide personalised guidance and support.

    - Method: Pair students with mentors or coaches who can offer advice, feedback, and support tailored to their career goals.

    - Example: A student interested in healthcare is paired with a mentor who works in the field, receiving guidance on coursework, internships, and career planning.

2. Work-Based Learning:

    - Purpose: To provide hands-on experience and practical skills.

- Method: Integrate work-based learning opportunities, such as internships or apprenticeships, into the curriculum.

- Example: A student in a business program completes an internship at a local company, gaining real-world experience and developing job-specific skills.

3. Technology Integration:

- Purpose: To enhance learning through digital tools and resources.

- Method: Use technology, such as online courses, simulations, and digital portfolios, to support skill development and career readiness.

- Example: Students use an online platform to complete industry-specific training modules and earn certifications that enhance their employability.

4. Peer Collaboration and Networking:

- Purpose: To build professional networks and collaborative skills.

- Method: Organise networking events, group projects, and peer mentoring programs.

- Example: Students attend a networking event where they can connect with professionals in their field of interest and practice their networking skills.

Scaffolding in secondary education and further education is essential for supporting students as they develop the skills and confidence needed for academic and career success. By providing structured support and gradually promoting independence, teachers can help students navigate complex tasks, develop critical thinking and problem-solving abilities, and become self-sufficient learners. Engaging parents, caregivers, and mentors in the scaffolding process further enhances its effectiveness, creating a collaborative and supportive learning environment. Through effective scaffolding strategies, students are better prepared to succeed in secondary education, further education, and beyond.

CHAPTER 6: SCAFFOLDING STUDENT QUESTIONS

When students express uncertainty or confusion, it's important to respond in a way that guides them towards finding the solution independently while providing the necessary support. Below are common questions students might ask and how to approach them using different scaffolding techniques.

QUESTION 1: "I DON'T KNOW WHAT TO DO."

Cueing and Prompting:

- Response: "What part of the instructions are you stuck on? Can you point out the step you're on?"

- Purpose: To help the student identify exactly where they are having trouble, encouraging them to focus on a specific aspect of the task.

Graphic Organisers:

- Response: "Let's look at your graphic organiser together. What part of the organiser have you filled out, and what comes next?"

- Purpose: To help the student use visual aids to see the structure of the task and determine the next steps.

Step-by-Step Instructions:

- Response: "Let's go through the checklist. Which step are you on, and what does it say you should do next?"

- Purpose: To break down the task into manageable steps, guiding the student to follow the sequence.

Modelling:

- Response: "Watch how I start this. First, I read the instructions carefully. Now, I'll show you how to do the first step."

- Purpose: To provide a clear example of how to begin the task, allowing the student to see the process in action.

Think-Aloud Strategies:

- Response: "I'm thinking aloud to show you how to approach this problem. First, I'll identify what I need to do. Next, I'll think about what information I have and what I need to find out."

- Purpose: To demonstrate the cognitive process involved in starting the task, helping the student develop similar thinking skills.

QUESTION 2: "IS THIS RIGHT?"

Cueing and Prompting:

- Response: "What makes you think it might be right or wrong? Can you explain your reasoning?"

- Purpose: To encourage the student to articulate their thought process and self-assess their work.

Peer Review:

- Response: "Why don't you compare your answer with a classmate and discuss why you think it's correct?"

- Purpose: To promote collaborative learning and peer feedback, helping the student validate their understanding through discussion.

Using Rubrics:

- Response: "Let's look at the rubric together. Does your work meet the criteria listed here?"

- Purpose: To provide clear expectations and criteria for self-assessment, guiding the student to evaluate their own work.

Think-Aloud Strategies:

- Response: "I'll think aloud as I check this. First, I'll look at the instructions again, then I'll compare it with my work."

- Purpose: To model the process of self-assessment, demonstrating how to cross-check work against instructions.

QUESTION 3: "I DON'T GET THIS."

Cueing and Prompting:

- Response: "Can you tell me what part is confusing? Is it the vocabulary, the instructions, or something else?"

- Purpose: To pinpoint the exact area of confusion, enabling more targeted support.

Graphic Organisers:

- Response: "Let's use a graphic organiser to break this down. What's the main idea, and what details do you need to understand?"

- Purpose: To visually organise information, helping the student see the relationships between different parts of the task.

Modelling:

- Response: "Watch as I work through this example. I'll explain each step as I go."

- Purpose: To show the student a practical demonstration of how to approach the problem.

Peer Support:

- Response: "Why don't you pair up with a classmate who understands this part? Maybe they can explain it in a different way."

- Purpose: To facilitate peer teaching, allowing the student to receive explanations in different words.

QUESTION 4: "WHAT DO I NEED TO DO NEXT?"

Cueing and Prompting:

- Response: "What was the last step you completed? What do the instructions say after that?"

- Purpose: To guide the student in following the sequence of steps outlined in the instructions.

Step-by-Step Instructions:

- Response: "Let's check the checklist. Which steps have you checked off, and what's the next one?"

- Purpose: To help the student see the logical progression of tasks.

Graphic Organisers:

- Response: "Look at your graphic organiser. What part have you filled in, and what's missing?"

- Purpose: To visually guide the student through the stages of the task.

Think-Aloud Strategies:

- Response: "I'm thinking aloud here. I've finished this part, so the next step is to..."

- Purpose: To model the thought process of identifying the next action.

QUESTION 5: "CAN YOU HELP ME?"

Cueing and Prompting:

- Response: "What have you tried so far? What do you think you could try next?"

- Purpose: To encourage the student to reflect on their efforts and consider additional strategies.

Graphic Organisers:

- Response: "Let's see what you have on your graphic organiser. What's missing or needs more detail?"

- Purpose: To help the student organise their thoughts and identify gaps in their understanding.

Step-by-Step Instructions:

- Response: "Sure, let's look at the steps again. Which step are you on, and what does it say you should do?"

- Purpose: To provide structured support, guiding the student through the task incrementally.

Modelling:

- Response: "Watch as I show you how to approach this problem. I'll explain my thinking as I go."

- Purpose: To demonstrate a clear example of how to tackle the task.

Think-Aloud Strategies:

- Response: "I'll think aloud while I work through this part. First, I consider what the problem is asking, then..."

- Purpose: To share the cognitive process, helping the student understand how to approach similar tasks independently.

QUESTION 6: "HOW DO I SPELL ___?"

Cueing and Prompting (Least Support)

- Response: "What sounds do you hear in the word? Try writing it down based on the sounds you can identify."

- Purpose: To encourage the student to use phonemic awareness and attempt to spell the word independently.

Using Reference Tools

- Response: "Have you checked the word wall or the dictionary?"

- Purpose: To prompt the student to use available resources to find the correct spelling, promoting self-reliance.

Chunking the Word

- Response: "Can you break the word into smaller parts or chunks? Think about the beginning, middle, and end sounds."

- Purpose: To help the student break the word into manageable segments, making it easier to spell.

Think-Aloud Strategies

- Response: "Let's think aloud together. If we want to spell 'elephant,' we start with the sounds: e-l-e-p-h-a-n-t. What letters can we use for each sound?"

- Purpose: To model the process of segmenting the word into sounds and matching them with letters.

Phonics Rules and Patterns

- Response: "Do you remember the rule for silent 'e' at the end of a word? How does that affect the spelling?"

- Purpose: To help the student apply phonics rules and patterns they have learned, aiding in spelling unfamiliar words.

Modelling (Most Support)

- Response: "Watch as I spell the word 'elephant.' E-l-e-p-h-a-n-t. Now you try it."

- Purpose: To provide a clear example for the student to follow, reinforcing correct spelling.

QUESTION 7: "WHY IS THIS IMPORTANT?"

Cueing and Prompting

- Response: "How do you think this skill or concept could be used in real life? Can you give an example?"
- Purpose: To help the student connect the lesson to real-world applications, enhancing relevance and motivation.

Providing Context

- Response: "This is important because it helps us understand how things work. For example, knowing fractions can help you divide a pizza equally among friends."
- Purpose: To provide a concrete example that illustrates the importance of the concept or skill.

Relating to Prior Knowledge

- Response: "Remember when we learned about this in our last unit? How does this build on what you already know?"
- Purpose: To connect the new information to prior knowledge, reinforcing its importance and context.

Think-Aloud Strategies

- Response: "I'm thinking about why this is important. If we understand this concept, it will help us solve more complex problems later on."
- Purpose: To model the process of considering the broader significance of a lesson, encouraging deeper thinking.

QUESTION 8: "I CAN'T FIND THE ANSWER IN THE TEXT."

Cueing and Prompting:

- Response: "What keywords did you use to search? Can you try rephrasing your question?"

- Purpose: To encourage the student to refine their search strategy.

Text Marking:

- Response: "Let's highlight important sections. Can you find any clues in the highlighted text?"

- Purpose: To help the student focus on relevant parts of the text.

Graphic Organisers:

- Response: "Use a T-chart to organise what you know and what you need to find."

- Purpose: To visually break down information and identify gaps.

QUESTION 9: "WHAT DOES THIS WORD MEAN?"

Cueing and Prompting:

- Response: "Can you use context clues from the surrounding sentences?"

- Purpose: To help the student infer the meaning from context.

Using Reference Tools:

- Response: "Have you checked a dictionary or thesaurus?"

- Purpose: To encourage the use of reference materials.

Think-Aloud Strategies:

- Response: "Let's think about similar words or roots. What does 'bio' usually mean?"

- Purpose: To model the process of breaking down and analysing word parts.

QUESTION 10: "HOW DO I START THIS ASSIGNMENT?"

Cueing and Prompting:

- Response: "What is the first instruction given? Can you explain it in your own words?"
- Purpose: To help the student understand the initial step.

Step-by-Step Instructions:

- Response: "Look at the first step on the checklist. What materials do you need?"
- Purpose: To provide a structured approach to beginning the task.

Modelling:

- Response: "Watch as I outline my introduction. How can you apply a similar structure?"
- Purpose: To provide a clear example to follow.

QUESTION 11: "WHAT IF I GET IT WRONG?"

Cueing and Prompting:

- Response: "What are some possible outcomes? How might you learn from a mistake?"
- Purpose: To encourage a growth mindset and risk-taking.

Think-Aloud Strategies:

- Response: "I'm thinking aloud about the risks and benefits. How might a mistake help me improve?"
- Purpose: To model reflective thinking and learning from errors.

Peer Review:

- Response: "Why don't you discuss your concerns with a classmate? They might have similar worries."
- Purpose: To normalise the fear of making mistakes and promote peer support.

QUESTION 12: "CAN I DO THIS DIFFERENTLY?"

Cueing and Prompting:

- Response: "What alternative approach are you considering? Can you explain why?"

- Purpose: To encourage creative thinking and justify choices.

Think-Aloud Strategies:

- Response: "I'm thinking about different methods. What are the pros and cons of each?"

- Purpose: To model decision-making and evaluating options.

Providing Flexibility:

- Response: "Yes, as long as you meet the criteria. How does your approach align with the goals?"

- Purpose: To allow autonomy while ensuring objectives are met.

QUESTION 13: "HOW MUCH DETAIL SHOULD I INCLUDE?"

Using Rubrics:

- Response: "Let's check the rubric. What does it say about detail?"

- Purpose: To use assessment criteria to guide the level of detail.

Cueing and Prompting:

- Response: "What key points do you think are most important?"

- Purpose: To help the student prioritise information.

Think-Aloud Strategies:

- Response: "I'm thinking about what to include by considering what's essential and what's extra."

- Purpose: To model the process of selecting relevant details.

QUESTION 14: "CAN I ASK FOR HELP FROM SOMEONE ELSE?"

Peer Support:

- Response: "Yes, you can ask a classmate. How can you explain what you need help with?"
- Purpose: To promote collaborative learning and communication skills.

Using Resources:

- Response: "Have you considered asking the librarian or using online forums?"
- Purpose: To encourage the use of diverse resources.

Self-Assessment:

- Response: "Before asking, can you try to summarise your question? This might clarify your thoughts."
- Purpose: To promote self-reflection and clearer communication.

QUESTION 15: "I'M FEELING OVERWHELMED."

Cueing and Prompting:

- Response: "What part of the task feels most difficult? Can you break it into smaller steps?"
- Purpose: To help the student manage tasks by chunking them.

Graphic Organisers:

- Response: "Let's use a mind map to organise your thoughts and tasks."
- Purpose: To visually organise and prioritise tasks.

Step-by-Step Instructions:

- Response: "Let's list the steps. Which one can you start with?"
- Purpose: To provide a clear, manageable starting point.

QUESTION 16: "HOW CAN I IMPROVE MY WORK?"

Using Rubrics:

- Response: "Look at the rubric. What areas need more work?"
- Purpose: To use clear criteria to guide improvement.

Peer Review:

- Response: "Ask a peer to give you feedback. What suggestions do they have?"
- Purpose: To benefit from peer feedback.

Think-Aloud Strategies:

- Response: "I'm thinking about feedback I've received. How can I apply it to make my work better?"
- Purpose: To model the process of using feedback constructively.

QUESTION 17: "WHY DO WE HAVE TO DO THIS?"

Providing Context:

- Response: "This activity helps us develop critical thinking skills. Can you think of a situation where these skills might be useful?"
- Purpose: To connect the task to real-life applications.

Relating to Prior Knowledge:

- Response: "Remember how we used similar skills in our last project? How did it help us then?"
- Purpose: To build on previous experiences.

Think-Aloud Strategies:

- Response: "I'm thinking about the purpose of this task. It seems to prepare us for..."
- Purpose: To model reflective thinking about the task's relevance.

QUESTION 18: "WHAT GRADE WILL I GET FOR THIS?"

Using Rubrics:

- Response: "Let's look at the rubric (mark scheme). Based on your work so far, what grade do you think you might get?"

- Purpose: To encourage self-assessment using clear criteria.

Cueing and Prompting:

- Response: "What elements of your work meet the highest standards? Which parts could be improved?"

- Purpose: To help the student identify strengths and areas for improvement.

Peer Review:

- Response: "Ask a classmate to assess your work using the rubric. What feedback do they provide?"

- Purpose: To incorporate peer assessment.

CHAPTER 7: FUTURE DIRECTIONS IN SCAFFOLDING AND TECHNOLOGY INTEGRATION

In today's educational landscape, technology plays an increasingly vital role in shaping how we teach and learn. This chapter explores the intersection of scaffolding and technology, highlighting how digital tools can enhance traditional scaffolding techniques and address the diverse needs of students. By integrating technology, educators can provide more personalised, adaptive, and engaging learning experiences that support students' academic growth and independence.

TECHNOLOGICAL ADVANCEMENTS AND SCAFFOLDING

Role of Digital Tools and Resources

Digital tools and resources have revolutionised scaffolding by offering scalable and adaptable support for students. Educational software, online platforms, and interactive simulations provide structured learning experiences tailored to individual needs. These technologies enable teachers to deliver just-in-time support, track student progress, and adjust instructional strategies based on real-time data.

Educational Software and Platforms

Platforms like Khan Academy, Duolingo, Moodle, and Google Classroom offer structured, adaptive learning experiences that scaffold student learning effectively. These tools provide interactive content, immediate feedback, and personalised learning paths, helping students progress at their own pace. For example:

- Khan Academy: Offers instructional videos and practice exercises that break down complex concepts into manageable steps.

- Duolingo: Uses gamification to scaffold language learning, providing immediate feedback and adjusting difficulty based on performance.

- Moodle and Google Classroom: Facilitate blended learning environments where teachers can scaffold lessons through multimedia resources, quizzes, and collaborative projects.

Benefits and Challenges of Technological Scaffolding

Benefits

- Personalisation and Adaptivity: Technology can tailor learning experiences to individual needs, providing targeted support and adjusting the level of difficulty based on student performance.

- Immediate Feedback: Digital tools offer instant feedback, helping students correct mistakes and reinforce learning promptly.

- Accessibility and Inclusivity: Features like text-to-speech, subtitles, and adjustable text sizes make learning materials more accessible to students with diverse needs.

- Increased Engagement: Interactive and gamified content keeps students engaged and motivated, promoting active learning and sustained interest.

Challenges

- Digital Divide: Unequal access to technology can exacerbate existing educational inequalities, with some students lacking the necessary devices or internet connectivity.

- Distractions and Overreliance: Technology can be a source of distraction, and overreliance on digital tools may hinder the development of critical thinking and problem-solving skills.

- Quality and Effectiveness: The variability in the quality of educational software means that not all tools provide effective scaffolding. Educators must carefully select and evaluate digital resources.

- Technical Issues: Problems such as software glitches or connectivity issues can disrupt learning and frustrate students and teachers alike.

Best Practices for Integrating Technology in Scaffolding

Aligning Digital Tools with Learning Goals

To maximise the benefits of technology, it is crucial to align digital tools with specific learning objectives. Educators should select tools that complement and enhance traditional instructional methods, ensuring that technology supports rather than replaces effective teaching practices.

Training and Support

Providing adequate training for teachers and students is essential for the effective use of technology. Professional development opportunities can help educators integrate digital tools into their teaching strategies, while students need guidance on how to use these tools responsibly and effectively.

Monitoring and Evaluation

Regular assessment of the impact of digital tools on student learning is necessary to ensure their effectiveness. Teachers should gather data on student performance and engagement, using this information to make informed decisions about instructional adjustments and technology use.

Fostering Digital Literacy

Teaching students digital literacy skills is crucial for navigating the modern educational landscape. This includes understanding how to use technology responsibly, critically evaluating online information, and protecting their privacy and security online.

Primary Education: Interactive Whiteboards and Educational Apps

In a primary school setting, interactive whiteboards and educational apps can provide engaging scaffolding for literacy and numeracy skills. For example, apps that teach phonics through interactive games can help young learners build foundational reading skills, while math apps can reinforce basic arithmetic through visual and interactive exercises.

Secondary Education: Virtual Labs and Online Simulations

In secondary education, virtual labs and online simulations enhance understanding in science subjects. For instance, students can conduct virtual chemistry experiments, allowing them to explore chemical reactions safely and thoroughly. These tools provide scaffolding by guiding students through the scientific method and offering instant feedback on their hypotheses and results.

Further Education: Online Courses and Digital Portfolios

In further education, online courses and digital portfolios support vocational training and career readiness. Platforms like Coursera and LinkedIn Learning offer courses that scaffold learning in various fields, from IT to business management. Digital portfolios allow students to document their skills and accomplishments, providing a comprehensive view of their learning journey and enhancing their employability.

Future Innovations in Scaffolding

Artificial Intelligence (AI)

AI has the potential to transform scaffolding by providing real-time, personalised support based on student performance and learning patterns. Intelligent tutoring systems can adapt content to individual needs, offering targeted assistance and adjusting difficulty levels dynamically.

Adaptive Learning Technologies

Advanced algorithms in adaptive learning technologies adjust the difficulty of tasks and provide customised support, ensuring that students are continually challenged at an appropriate level. These technologies can identify areas where students struggle and offer additional practice or alternative explanations.

Virtual and Augmented Reality (VR/AR)

Emerging VR and AR technologies offer immersive learning experiences that scaffold complex concepts in an engaging manner. For example, VR can simulate historical events or scientific phenomena, allowing students to explore and interact with content in a way that enhances understanding and retention.

The integration of technology with scaffolding techniques represents a significant advancement in educational practices, offering new opportunities to enhance student learning and engagement. By thoughtfully incorporating digital tools, educators can provide personalised, adaptive support that meets the diverse needs of their students. As technology continues to evolve, it will be essential for educators to stay informed about emerging tools and strategies, ensuring that scaffolding practices remain effective and relevant. Through continuous adaptation and innovation, we can prepare students for success in an increasingly digital world, fostering lifelong learning and achievement.

About the Author

Abigail Hawkins – The Driving Force Behind Inclusive Education

With over 30 years of experience, Abigail Hawkins stands as a seasoned and passionate SENCO, renowned for her commitment to advancing Special Educational Needs (SEN) provisions. As the founder of SENDCO Solutions and SENsible SENCO CIC, Abigail leverages her extensive expertise to offer invaluable support and guidance to educators and schools nationwide.

A Champion for All Learners

Abigail's vast experience spans a diverse range of subjects, addressing the needs of students from toddlers to adults. Her practical approach to SEN issues is underscored by a wealth of consultancy work, where she collaborates with leading software and product companies to pioneer innovative tools for SEN support. Her efforts extend to designing and delivering teaching assistant apprenticeship and master's degree programs, as well as authoring several books and resources on SEN and exclusions. Additionally, Abigail provides comprehensive support to schools through detailed reviews, targeted training sessions, and ongoing consultancy to ensure the effective implementation of SEN strategies.

Leading a Thriving Network

As the founder of a support network that empowers nearly 13,000 SENCOs, Abigail is dedicated to fostering connections and sharing vital resources. Her impactful tenure as the Chair of Governors for three schools in the East Midlands highlights her unwavering commitment to educational leadership.

Pioneering Beyond Traditional Channels

Abigail's influence transcends traditional educational frameworks. During the challenging lockdown periods, she was a key figure in hosting a series of SEN webinars that reached a global audience exceeding 60,000 viewers. Embracing modern communication methods, she also manages a successful YouTube channel, making SEN-related information both accessible and engaging.

A Relentless Advocate for Inclusive Education

Abigail's non-nonsense, hands-on approach enables her to make a significant impact in the lives of countless students, educators, and schools. Her steadfast dedication to inclusive education remains evident through her continuous efforts to promote and implement effective SEN strategies.

Becoming a subscriber to SEnsible SENCo offers a wealth of advantages designed to support and enhance your role as an SEN professional. As a member, you will gain:

- **Exclusive Access to Resources**: Unlock a treasure trove of expertly curated materials, including guides, templates, and best practice strategies tailored specifically for SEN coordinators and educators.

- **Cutting-Edge Insights**: Stay ahead with the latest developments in SEN research, policy updates, and innovative teaching methods through our regularly updated content and newsletters.

- **Professional Development**: Benefit from comprehensive training modules, webinars, and workshops that provide valuable CPD opportunities, helping you to refine your skills and knowledge.

- **Community Support**: Join a vibrant community of like-minded professionals, sharing experiences, advice, and support through our forums and networking events.

These QFT booklets have been distributed to subscribers as an online version and they can easily access the videos that accompany.

www.sensiblesenco.org.uk

Printed in Great Britain
by Amazon

46184049R00097